ERIC THEISS

LOVIN' YOUR AIR FRYER

110 FAST & EASY RECIPES FOR MORNIN' TO LATE-NIGHT MUNCHIN'

Post Hill
PRESS

SENDIN' SHOUT OUTS TO MY PEOPLE

I want to thank my wife Jesse for being by my side during this entire process and helping me survive the boring parts, and my sons Cam and Max for their clever ideas and fun word play. My culinary friends Karen Miller, Lynn Willis, and Kris Amerine jumped into my think tank and always came up strong! To the team at Post Hill Press, including Anthony Zacardi, Megan Wheeler, and Allison Griffith, for supporting this launch. Lastly, to Linda Lisco—thank you so much for directing this ship to a nice, soft landing—and to Amy Nichols for being my creative eyes on the ground. I am very appreciative of everyone involved in this fun cookbook project.

GETTIN' TO KNOW ERIC

Eric Theiss's culinary interests started as a child when his Italian mother gave him his first cookbook at 6... and from there, he never stopped cooking.

Chef Eric Theiss was born and raised in New Jersey, and his culinary interests started as a child when his Italian mother would encourage him to cook and investigate food and fine dining throughout his young adult life. During his early twenties, after studies led him to a typical office "day job," Eric's love of fine dining drew him out to work long nights at Culinary Renaissance, where he had the opportunity to train under the acclaimed chef, Frank Falcinelli.

In 1997 he opened his own fine dining restaurant and bar called Meritage in West Chester, Pennsylvania, which earned rave reviews from prominent Philadelphia food critics.

CREATING COOKING SUCCESS AT HOME

While ever the budding restaurateur, Eric began to have reoccurring conversations with guests and discovered that they shared his love for cooking, but needed help to make home cooking less complicated, more accessible, and most importantly, tasty. Here is when his interest in kitchen product innovation started, and Eric began working with kitchen brands and retailers to demystify cooking at home, making him one of the leading cooking equipment gurus in the industry.

For the past 15 years, Eric has showcased his own collections as well as curated collections of kitchen equipment

and cookbooks on shopping networks, national morning shows, infomercials, broadcast and cable TV, and live streaming platforms.

ERIC IS AS APPROACHABLE AS HIS RECIPES

Eric's love for cooking, teaching, and "culinary inventing" is as approachable as his energetic personality. His straightforward, no-nonsense approach to cooking has helped millions of people be successful in the kitchen with fresh ideas on food that range from everyday meals to comfort- food creations and special occasion masterpieces. With nearly 1,000,000 cookbooks sold, Eric is excited to launch *Lovin' Your Air Fryer*, a new series of books that will surprise readers and get them asking, "You can make that in an air fryer?"

When Eric's not in the kitchen or TV studio, he is at home in Pennsylvania with his brilliant wife Jessica and their teenage sons Cameron and Maxwell, who often make cameo appearances with Eric on Facebook Live and IGTV. Ever the animal lovers, the family cats PoePoe, Whitman, and Ginger get the benefit of living in a home filled with love and really good food.

FOLLOW ERIC:
- Facebook: @EricTheissTV
- Instagram: @erictheiss
- TikTok: @erictheissTV
- YouTube: @TheEricTheiss
- Website: erictheiss.com

LOVIN' YOUR AIR FRYER AGAIN— OR JUST GETTIN' STARTED?

Several years ago when air frying first arrived on the scene, it seemed like a cool idea or a new trend. Now, air frying has been elevated to a true cooking technique, respected and loved by so many. Air frying allows us to cook with super-heated cyclonic air instead of oil; you are cooking in a vat of air instead of a vat of oil! This can save us up to 70% of calories from fat. Undoubtedly a healthier way to fry, air frying technology has come so far and there are air fryers to suit every lifestyle. People always tell me they bought their air fryer to enjoy basic fried foods like onion rings and French fries but come to love their air fryer for something as simple and healthy as salmon filets or as elaborate as a Beef Wellington. How cool is that?! I hope this book helps you to discover all of the different ways to air fry all of your favorite foods.

HEALTHIER CRUNCHIN': AIR FRYIN' TIPS AND TRICKS

• If you like things extra crispy, use either a nonstick spray or an oil sprayer to add just a light layer of oil to the outside of your foods. I recommend an oil sprayer because you can choose your favorite oil to fill it with. They do make high quality cans of oil sprayers now along with traditional nonstick sprays cans. Another alternative is to toss the food in a bowl of 1 tablespoon of oil to coat. This doesn't work with freshly breaded foods, and you'll want to use one of the oil sprayers for that. Tossing is better for frozen foods.

• Double Dip! If you are dredging or breading foods, try giving it an extra dip back into the egg mixture and then back into the crumbs in order to add an extra thick and crispy layer to your foods.

• Give your food some space: Air fryers need adequate space for air flow to help foods crisp up and also to ensure more even cooking.

• Preheating is great! While it's almost

never absolutely necessary to preheat the air fryer, preheating the air fryer for 1 to 2 minutes can help jump start the cooking process and seal in the crunch! It also helps proteins not to stick to the basket or rack.

• During cooking, it's always a good idea to flip your food halfway or give it a shake to move things around for more even cooking.

• A favorite way of mine to get extra golden proteins is to blend your spices with mayonnaise and then brush them onto the food.

• If you have an air fryer with a basket or an oven style air fryer with air flow racks, it can be beneficial to spray them with oil or nonstick spray prior to cooking, especially if you're cooking proteins that may stick naturally when heated.

• Any oven-proof vessel can be used in any air fryer. Whether it's metal, ceramic or stoneware, as long as it fits inside your fryer and does not come close to touching the top heating element, it will work!

• Air fryers save time in two ways: 1. A standard oven takes about 15 minutes to heat up to 400°F. With your air fryer, you do not need to preheat it, so you're already 15 minutes ahead of the game. 2. Air fryers cook more efficiently thanks to a very large fan in a very confined space.

• When cooking frozen foods, a rule of thumb is to take about 5 min off the time box on the package and check for doneness then. Use the same temperature the food packaging recommends.

• To batter or to bread? If you want to coat your food with some sort of breading, make sure you use the DRY, WET, DRY dredging method because if you try to batter your food, it will drip down and create a mess inside of your air fryer. If there is a batter you love to use, you can use it by freezing the battered food before air frying it.

TABLE OF CONTENTS

SWEET & SAVORY
MORNINGS

APPLE-WALNUT DUTCH BABY

SERVES 4 TO 6

INGREDIENTS

Cooking spray

4 tablespoons butter

3 tablespoons brown sugar

2 medium apples, diced

½ cup chopped walnuts

¾ cup flour

2 tablespoons granulated sugar, divided

¼ teaspoon baking powder

½ teaspoon salt

¼ + ⅛ teaspoon cinnamon

⅛ teaspoon nutmeg

4 eggs, beaten

¾ cup milk

Whipped cream for serving (optional)

DIRECTIONS

1 Spray a deep 9-inch nonstick round cake pan, 8×8 -inch deep nonstick baking pan, or round baking pan that fits into the air fryer with cooking spray.

2 Melt butter in the pan at 350°F for 3 minutes. Once the butter is melted, stir in the brown sugar, apples, and walnuts. Using an oven mitt or tongs, carefully remove the pan from the air fryer and set aside.

3 In a large bowl, combine flour, 1 tablespoon of the granulated sugar, baking powder, salt, the ¼ teaspoon cinnamon, and nutmeg. Add eggs and milk to the dry ingredients and whisk until the batter is smooth.

4 Pour batter over the apples and walnuts and place the pan back into the air fryer. If using an oven-style model, place the pan on the bottom rack. Cook at 350°F for 20 minutes.

5 While the pancake is cooking, combine the remaining 1 tablespoon granulated sugar and ⅛ teaspoon cinnamon; set aside.

6 At the end of the cooking time, use an oven mitt to remove the pan from the air fryer. Invert the pancake onto a serving plate. Sprinkle the top with the cinnamon-sugar mixture and whipped cream, if using.

> **ERIC SAYS:** Top this with chocolate syrup and powdered sugar to make a delicious dessert!

EL DENVER QUICHE

SERVES 4 TO 6

INGREDIENTS

- 6 eggs
- ¼ cup heavy cream
- ½ cup salsa
- ¼ teaspoon cumin
- 2 tablespoons fresh cilantro, chopped
- Salt and pepper
- 1 (9-inch) prepared pie crust (in a pan)
- 1 pound chorizo, cooked and cooled
- ½ cup chopped green peppers, sautéed and cooled
- ½ cup chopped onion, sautéed and cooled
- 1 cup shredded Monterrey jack cheese
- 1 cup shredded Manchego cheese

DIRECTIONS

1 In a medium bowl, whisk together the eggs, cream, salsa, cumin, cilantro, and salt and pepper to taste. Lay the chorizo, peppers, onions, and cheeses in the crust. Pour egg mixture over the top.

2 Cook at 325°F for about 25 to 30 minutes or until eggs are set.

3 Cool for 10 to 15 minutes before cutting.

CALIFORNIA BRUNCH TOMATOES

SERVES 6

INGREDIENTS

Cooking spray

6 medium tomatoes

Salt and pepper

1 cup shredded Swiss cheese

1 cup chopped cooked turkey

6 eggs

2 avocados, seeded and diced

1 cup baby arugula or baby spinach

1 tablespoon fresh lime juice

2 tablespoon chopped fresh cilantro

DIRECTIONS

1 Spray a 9-inch round baking dish or pan with cooking spray. Cut the tops off the tomatoes and scoop out the seeds. Season inside of tomatoes with salt and pepper and place them in the prepared pan.

2 Evenly divide the cheese and turkey among the tomatoes. Crack one egg into each tomato. Cook at 325°F for about 20 to 25 minutes or until eggs are desired doneness.

3 Using a serving spoon, transfer tomatoes from dish (they will be soft) to plates.

4 In a medium bowl, combine the diced avocados, arugula, and lime juice. Season with salt and pepper to taste.

5 Serve tomatoes with arugula mixture, topped with chopped cilantro.

ERIC SAYS: This makes a great appetizer too. For an added crunch, add crushed tortilla chips or strips.

HONEY-CINNAMON GRANOLA

MAKES ABOUT 3 CUPS

INGREDIENTS

- 3 tablespoons butter
- 1 tablespoon water
- 3 tablespoons honey
- ½ teaspoon vanilla extract
- 1 cup whole oats
- ½ cup sweetened coconut flakes
- 2 tablespoons raw sunflower seeds
- 2 tablespoons raw pumpkin seeds
- ¾ cup chopped pecans or walnuts
- 1 tablespoon flax seed
- ½ teaspoon cinnamon
- ½ cup dried cranberries or raisins

DIRECTIONS

1 In an 8-inch round baking pan, combine the butter, water, honey, and vanilla extract. Heat at 340°F until butter is melted, about 4 minutes.

2 Meanwhile, in a medium bowl, combine the oats, coconut, sunflower seeds, pumpkin seeds, nuts, flax seed, and cinnamon.

3 Using an oven mitt, remove the melted butter from the air fryer and pour over the oats. Mix well, ensuring that the butter mixing is evenly coating the dry ingredients.

4 Return the mixture to the pan and cook at 340°F for 15 minutes, stirring the granola every 5 minutes.

5 Using an oven mitt, remove granola from air fryer and stir in dried fruit.

6 Let cool and store in an air-tight container.

> **ERIC SAYS:** Try this served with vanilla ice cream!

BREAKFAST SAUSAGE STRATA

SERVES 4 TO 6

INGREDIENTS

Cooking spray

4 to 5 cups cubed challah bread (1-inch)

1 cup cooked breakfast sausage

½ cup frozen chopped spinach, thawed and squeezed dry

½ cup sautéed onion

½ cup chopped roasted red pepper

2 cups shredded Swiss cheese, divided

6 eggs

¼ cup milk

¼ cup half and half

¼ teaspoon red pepper flakes

Salt and pepper

DIRECTIONS

1 Spray an 8-inch baking dish or round pan with nonstick cooking spray.

2 Layer bread, sausage, spinach, onion, roasted pepper, and half of the cheese in the pan.

3 In a bowl, whisk together the eggs, milk, half and half, red pepper flakes, and salt and pepper to taste. Pour evenly over layers in the baking dish.

4 Cover with foil and place in the air fryer. Cook at 325°F for about 15 to 20 minutes or until eggs are set.

5 Remove foil. Sprinkle remaining cheese on top. Cook, uncovered, at 325°F for an additional 5 minutes or until cheese is melted and browned.

ERIC SAYS: Try a brioche bread for a delicious twist on this recipe.

SOUTHERN STUFFED BISCUITS

MAKES 6

INGREDIENTS

4 eggs

Salt and pepper

1 can refrigerated biscuit dough (6 biscuits)

¼ cup hot pepper jelly

1 cup shredded Cheddar cheese

1 cup diced ham

Cooking spray

1 egg yolk + 2 teaspoons water

1 tablespoon "everything" seasoning

DIRECTIONS

1 In a medium bowl, whisk eggs with salt and pepper to taste and cook in a skillet to a soft scramble. Set aside to cool.

2 Open biscuits and separate. Press each one flat to a ¼ inch-thickness. Top biscuits with pepper jelly, scrambled eggs, cheese and ham. Fold the layered biscuits in half and pinch to close.

3 Spray the air fryer basket or shelves with cooking spray and place biscuits in the air fryer. In a small bowl, whisk egg yolk and water together and brush top of biscuits with the egg wash. Sprinkle with everything seasoning.

4 Cook at 350°F for about 10 to 15 minutes or until browned.

WHITE GRAVY: In a saucepan, melt 3 tablespoons butter. Whisk in 3 tablespoons flour. Cook and stir for about 2 minutes. Slowly whisk in 2 cups milk. Add 1 cup chicken stock, 1 sprig thyme, 1 bay leaf, a pinch of salt and 1 teaspoon cracked black pepper. Cook, stirring frequently, for about 20 minutes on low, until thickened.

> **ERIC SAYS:** Serve this with white gravy to bring out that extra Southern feel.

ENCHILADAS HUEVOS VERDES

MAKES 6 ENCHILADAS

INGREDIENTS

Cooking spray

½ cup frozen chopped spinach, thawed and squeezed dry

½ cup chopped cooked broccoli

½ cup chopped onion, sautéed

½ cup chopped green pepper, sautéed

2 cups shredded Monterey Jack cheese

6 flour tortillas

6 eggs

½ cup salsa verde

¼ cup fresh cilantro, chopped

DIRECTIONS

1 Spray an 8-inch round baking dish or pan with cooking spray.

2 In a bowl, mix together spinach, broccoli, onion, green pepper, and half of the cheese. Divide mixture evenly among the tortillas and roll tightly. Place tortillas in prepared dish.

3 Whisk together eggs, salsa, and cilantro. Pour evenly over the tortillas.

4 Cover dish with foil and place in the air fryer. Cook at 350°F for about 15 to 20 minutes until eggs are cooked.

5 Carefully remove foil and sprinkle remaining cheese on top. Cook 5 more minutes.

BLOODY MARY: Mix 1 shot vodka, 3 ounces Clamato juice, 1 teaspoon lemon juice, 2 dashes Worcestershire sauce, 2 dashes red pepper sauce, ¼ teaspoon celery salt, ¼ teaspoon ground black pepper, 1 tablespoon horseradish, and pour over ice. Serve garnished with a celery stick, olive, and pickle spear.

> **ERIC SAYS:** This enchilada dish pairs well with a Bloody Mary cocktail. Try one of my favorite recipes.

RASPBERRY CHEESECAKE BREAKFAST BREAD PUDDINGS

SERVES 6

INGREDIENTS

- 2 ounces cream cheese, room temperature
- 2 tablespoons sugar, divided
- 1 teaspoon vanilla extract, divided
- 2 eggs
- ⅓ cup milk
- 5 slices cinnamon swirl bread, cut into ½-inch pieces
- Cooking spray
- 1½ tablespoon seedless raspberry jam
- 6 stand alone muffin cups
- Maple syrup for serving

DIRECTIONS

1 In a small bowl, combine the cream cheese, 1 tablespoon of the sugar, and ½ teaspoon of the vanilla until smooth.

2 In a large bowl, whisk the eggs, milk, remaining sugar and vanilla extract well combined. Add the bread to the egg mixture and toss to coat evenly.

3 Spray 6 standard muffin cups with cooking spray and fill each about halfway with the bread mixture. Divide the cream cheese mixture among the muffin cups, placing it in the middle of the bread mixture. Divide the jam among the muffin cups, placing on the cream cheese. Use the rest of the bread mixture to cover the cream cheese and jam, making sure the muffin cups are evenly filled.

4 Preheat air fryer for 2 minutes at 340°F.

5 Using an oven mitt, place the muffin cups in the air fryer and cook for 10 minutes.

6 Serve with warm maple syrup.

> **ERIC SAYS:** Bread pudding is always better when the bread has become stale first. If you don't have stale bread, toast the bread to harden it some.

CHOCOLATE CHIP-WALNUT BAKED OATMEAL

SERVES 2

INGREDIENTS

- ¾ cup whole oats
- 3 tablespoons light brown sugar
- ½ teaspoon cinnamon
- ¾ teaspoon baking powder
- 3 tablespoons mini chocolate chips
- ¼ cup chopped walnuts
- ¼ cup milk
- ½ cup water
- 1 egg, beaten
- 1 teaspoon vanilla extract
- Cooking spray

DIRECTIONS

1 In a medium bowl, combine oats, brown sugar, cinnamon, baking powder, chocolate chips, and walnuts. Stir in the milk, water, egg and vanilla and mix well.

2 Preheat air fryer for 2 minutes to 350°F for 2 minutes.

3 While the air fryer is preheating, spray two 8-ounce ramekins with cooking spray. Divide the mixture evenly between the ramekins.

4 Using an oven mitt, place the ramekins in the air fryer. Cook at 350°F for 20 minutes. Serve warm.

> **ERIC SAYS:** This is delicious served with fresh berries and whipped cream.

LOADED TATER BAKE

SERVES 4 TO 6

INGREDIENTS

Cooking spray

5 cups tater tots, cooked according to package instructions

1 cup grape tomatoes, halved

¾ cup crisp-cooked chopped bacon, divided

2 cups shredded Cheddar cheese

6 eggs

½ cup sour cream

Salt and pepper

¼ cup scallions, chopped

DIRECTIONS

1 Spray an 8x8-inch baking dish or pan with cooking spray.

2 Arrange the cooked tots in the pan. Top with tomatoes, ½ cup of the bacon, and half of the cheese.

3 Whisk together the eggs, sour cream, and salt and pepper to taste. Pour over ingredients in pan.

4 Cover dish with foil. Cook at 350°F for about 15 to 20 minutes, until eggs are cooked.

5 Remove foil and top with the scallions, remaining ¼ cup bacon, and remaining cheese. Cook for another 5 minutes, until cheese is lightly browned.

> **ERIC SAYS:** Tots are so versatile—you can top them with so many different ingredients! Try salsa and guacamole and call them "TOT-CHOS!"

GREEN EGGS & HAM BREAKFAST NAAN

SERVES 4

INGREDIENTS

¾ cup prepared pesto

4 pieces naan bread

2 cups shredded mozzarella cheese

4 ounces prosciutto, cut into ribbons

Cooking spray

4 egg whites, whipped

Salt and pepper

2 cups baby arugula

2 tablespoons fresh basil, chopped

DIRECTIONS

1 Spread one-quarter of the pesto on each piece of naan bread. Top with the mozzarella and prosciutto.

2 Spray air fryer shelves or basket with cooking spray. Carefully place naan on the shelves or in the basket. Top each naan with one-quarter of the whipped egg whites and season with salt and pepper.

3 Cook at 350°F for about 8 minutes or until the egg white is cooked through.

4 Top with arugula and basil and serve immediately.

ERIC SAYS: If you don't like prosciutto, you can substitute any other cooked and chopped breakfast meat. This also works great on a prepared pizza crust.

CONFETTI TEA BISCUITS

MAKES ABOUT 12

INGREDIENTS

1¾ cup all-purpose flour

⅓ cup sugar

¼ teaspoon baking soda

1 teaspoon baking powder

½ cup multicolored sprinkles

2 tablespoons butter, melted

1½ teaspoons vanilla extract

1 egg, beaten

¼ cup + 1 tablespoon milk

DIRECTIONS

1 In a medium bowl, combine the flour, sugar, baking soda, baking powder and 3 tablespoons of the sprinkles in a bowl. Combine the butter, egg, vanilla, and milk in a small bowl.

2 Add the wet ingredients to the dry ingredients and stir gently just until well-combined. Shape the dough into 1½-tablespoon-sized balls. Roll each dough ball in the remaining sprinkles and set aside.

3 Preheat air fryer for 2 minutes at 375°F. 6 Line rack or basket with parchment paper. Place biscuits in fryer and cook for 8 to 10 minutes or until lightly golden. (Cook in batches if necessary.) Cool on a wire rack.

ORANGE CRANBERRY SCONES

MAKES 8

INGREDIENTS

FOR THE SCONES

2 cups baking mix

¼ cup flour

¼ cup sugar

1 tablespoon orange zest

¾ cup dried cranberries

6 tablespoons butter, frozen for 15 minutes

1 large egg, beaten

⅓ cup milk

1 teaspoon vanilla extract

FOR THE GLAZE

1½ teaspoons orange juice

½ teaspoon water

½ cup powdered sugar

DIRECTIONS

1 **For the scones:** In a large bowl, combine the baking mix, flour, sugar, orange zest, and cranberries. Using the large-hole side of a cheese grater, grate the butter into the mixture. Gently toss to combine.

2 In a separate bowl, whisk the egg, milk, and vanilla. Fold the wet ingredients into dry ingredients, being careful not to overmix. Knead the mixture to bring the dough together.

3 Form the dough into a 7-inch circle. Cut into eight wedges.

4 Place the wedges on a parchment paper-lined air fryer rack or basket. If using an oven-model, place on the bottom shelf. Cook at 365°F for 15 minutes. Remove from air fryer and cool on a wire rack.

5 **For the glaze:** Right before serving, stir together the orange juice, water, and powdered sugar and drizzle over scones.

> **ERIC SAYS:** Freshen up your leftover scones by toasting and spreading butter and jelly on top.

STRAWBERRIES & CREAM DANISH TWISTS

MAKES 12

INGREDIENTS

Parchment paper

3 ounces cream cheese, room temperature

1 tablespoon + 1 teaspoon granulated sugar

½ teaspoon vanilla extract

1 tube refrigerator crescent dough sheet

3 tablespoons strawberry jam

½ cup powdered sugar

1 tablespoon water

DIRECTIONS

1 Line an air fryer rack or basket with parchment paper.

2 In a small bowl, combine the cream cheese, sugar, and vanilla extract; stir until smooth.

3 Unroll the crescent dough on a lightly floured surface. Spread the cream cheese mixture over the bottom half. Spread the jam over the cream cheese mixture. Fold the top half of the dough over the filling and lightly pinch to keep the filling in.

4 With a paring knife or pizza cutter, cut the dough into 12 equal strips. Twist each strip 3 to 4 times and place on rack or in basket.

5 Place 6 strips on a rack or in the basket (don't overcrowd the basket) and cook at 375°F for 6 minutes. With an oven mitt or tongs, remove cooked twists. Repeat process with remaining strips. Let cool.

6 In a small bowl, stir together the powdered sugar and water. Drizzle over twists before serving.

> **ERIC SAYS:** I love lemon curd on so many pastries! Substituting lemon curd for the strawberry jam gives it a slightly tart taste. To take it to another level, try substituting the cream cheese with crème fraîche, which a lot of supermarkets now sell ready made!

SHRIMP SCAMPI FRITTATA

SERVES 4 TO 6

INGREDIENTS

Cooking spray

1 cup cooked spaghetti

1 cup chopped cooked shrimp

½ cup sliced onions, caramelized

1 cup shredded mozzarella

6 eggs

½ cup heavy cream

1 tablespoon minced garlic

3 tablespoons chopped fresh parsley

Salt and pepper

8 cherry tomatoes, halved

¼ cup grated Parmesan cheese

DIRECTIONS

1 Spray an 8-inch baking dish or pan with cooking spray.

2 Layer the spaghetti, shrimp, caramelized onions, and mozzarella in the baking dish.

3 In a bowl, whisk together the eggs, cream, garlic, parsley, and salt and pepper to taste. Pour the egg mixture evenly over the spaghetti and top with the tomatoes. Cover the dish with foil and cook at 325°F for about 25 to 30 minutes.

4 Carefully remove the foil and sprinkle with Parmesan cheese. Cook for an additional 3 to 5 minutes or until cheese is browned.

MIMOSAS: In a champagne flute, combine 1 ounce chilled orange vodka, 1 ounce lemon juice, 1 ounce orange juice, and 3 ounces chilled Champagne.

ERIC SAYS: Why not serve this with mimosas?

SAVORY BRUNCH POTATOES

SERVES 4 TO 6

INGREDIENTS

- 2 pounds baby red potatoes, quartered
- 2 tablespoons olive oil
- ¼ teaspoon fennel seed
- ¼ teaspoon ground sage
- 1 tablespoon capers, smashed
- 1 tablespoon paprika
- ¼ teaspoon garlic powder
- ¼ teaspoon dried thyme
- ¼ teaspoon onion powder
- ¼ teaspoon salt
- ¼ teaspoon ground black pepper
- Zest of one lemon
- 2 tablespoons fresh parsley, chopped
- 2 tablespoons butter
- Cooking spray

DIRECTIONS

1 In a large bowl, toss the potatoes with all the ingredients except lemon zest, parsley, and butter.

2 Spray air fryer shelves or basket with cooking spray.

3 Place the potatoes in the air fryer and cook on 400°F for about 20 to 30 minutes or until tender, rotating the racks or shaking the basket halfway through the cooking time.

4 Transfer potatoes from the air fryer to a serving bowl. Toss with lemon zest, butter, and parsley.

ERIC SAYS: Take the flavors up a notch by adding crumbled cooked breakfast sausage at breakfast or crumbled cooked Italian sausage at dinner time!

SMALL BITES
YOU'RE NOT SHARIN'

BACON & BLUE CHEESE-STUFFED BUFFALO SHRIMP

MAKES 16 SHRIMP

INGREDIENTS

- 1 cup crumbled blue cheese
- ½ cup cooked and finely crumbled bacon
- 16 jumbo shrimp, shelled, deveined, with tails on
- 2 large eggs
- ¾ cup Buffalo sauce, divided
- ¾ cup almond flour
- 1 teaspoon salt
- ½ teaspoon pepper
- 2 cups finely crushed hot sauce pork rinds
- 1 teaspoon garlic powder
- 1 teaspoon dried parsley flakes
- Cooking spray

DIRECTIONS

1 In a small bowl, combine blue cheese and bacon. Mix well and set aside.

2 Using a small, sharp knife, cut a deep pocket into the back of each shrimp, being careful not to cook completely through. Stuff a small amount of the blue cheese and bacon mixture into the shrimp, then tightly press into shrimp. Continue the same process with all remaining shrimp.

3 In a small bowl, beat eggs and ½ cup of the hot sauce. Then, in a shallow dish, combine the almond flour, salt, and pepper. In a second shallow dish, mix the pork rinds, garlic powder, and dried parsley.

4 Dip each side of the shrimp first into flour mixture, then into the egg mixture, then into the pork rinds. Dip shrimp back to egg mixture, and then again into the pork rinds. Place dipped shrimp on a tray or plate. Repeat the process for the rest of the shrimp.

5 Spray the air fryer racks or basket with cooking spray. Arrange half of the shrimp in the air fryer as far as possible from one another. Cook at 375°F for 10 minutes or until crispy and golden brown, turning shrimp halfway through cooking time. Repeat with remaining shrimp. Drizzle with remaining ¼ cup Buffalo sauce.

> **ERIC SAYS:** This recipe calls for what I like to call the "double dip" method of dredging. With air frying, this method of double coating the food makes the end result even crispier!

CIDER HOUSE WINGS

SERVES 8 TO 10

INGREDIENTS

FOR THE SAUCE

- 4 cups fresh apple cider
- 3 tablespoons butter
- 1 teaspoon fresh cracked black pepper

FOR THE WINGS

- 3 pounds chicken wings
- 1 tablespoon canola oil
- 1 teaspoon Chinese 5 spice powder
- Cooking spray
- Ranch or blue cheese dressing for serving

DIRECTIONS

1 For the sauce: In a saucepan, bring the cider to a boil, then reduce heat to simmer. Cook, stirring frequently, for 10 to 15 minutes or until reduced to ¾ cup. Remove from heat and whisk in butter and pepper. Set aside.

2 Preheat air fryer to 400°F. Toss chicken wings in oil and 5 spice powder. Spray air fryer racks or basket with cooking spray. Place chicken in air fryer and cook for 20 to 25 minutes, turning wings halfway through the cooking time. (Cook in batches if necessary.)

3 Place cooked wings in a large bowl and toss wings with sauce. Serve with ranch or blue cheese dressing.

> **ERIC SAYS:** Adding Korean gochujang chili paste, fresh cilantro, and a little fresh ginger to the sauce brings an Asian flair to the wings!

CAROLINA CHICKEN CRISPY SUSHI

MAKES 2 ROLLS (12 PIECES)

INGREDIENTS

- 2 sheets of nori (dried edible seaweed for sushi)
- 1½ cups cooked sticky rice
- 1 cup shredded cooked chicken
- 3 tablespoons barbecue sauce
- ¼ cup chopped dill pickles
- 2 Colby Jack cheese sticks
- 2 eggs, beaten
- 1 cup all-purpose flour
- 2 cups panko breadcrumbs
- Cooking spray
- ½ cup prepared Asian-style dipping sauce

DIRECTIONS

1 Lay the nori sheets on a work surface. Carefully spread ¾ cup rice on the bottom two-thirds of each nori sheet.

2 In a bowl, mix chicken and BBQ sauce and place an equal amount on top of the rice. Top the chicken with pickles and cheese sticks. Tightly roll up. Slice each roll into 6 pieces.

3 Create a dredging station with flour in a bowl; eggs in a second bowl, and panko breadcrumbs in a third bowl. Lightly dust each sushi piece with flour, dip in the egg, then flour, then egg, then panko. Place dipped rolls on a plate or tray and repeat the process for remaining pieces.

4 Spray air fryer shelves or basket with cooking spray. Place sushi air fryer and spray with cooking spray. Cook at 400°F for 8 minutes or until browned and crisp, turning them halfway through the cooking process.

5 Serve with dipping sauce.

> **ERIC SAYS:** You can literally swap out the chicken for anything! Tofu, avocado, pulled pork, cooked shrimp...options are endless!

ORANGE CHICKEN WONTONS

MAKES 18 TO 20

INGREDIENTS

- 1 cup chopped cooked chicken
- 4 ounces cream cheese
- 1 cup shredded mozzarella cheese
- 2 tablespoons orange marmalade
- ⅛ teaspoon cayenne pepper
- 18 to 20 wonton wrappers
- Cooking spray
- Sweet and sour sauce for serving

DIRECTIONS

1 In a medium bowl, stir together chicken, cream cheese, mozzarella, marmalade, and cayenne.

2 Lay wonton wrappers out on a work surface. Spoon 1 to 2 teaspoons filling in the center of each wonton. Lightly moisten 2 edges of the wrappers with water. Fold over corner to corner making a triangle. Press edges closed.

3 Spray air fryer shelves or basket with cooking spray. Arrange wontons in fryer. Spray wontons lightly with cooking spray. Cook at 400°F for about 8 minutes, turning halfway through the cooking time and spraying lightly with cooking spray.

4 Serve with sweet and sour sauce.

ERIC SAYS: You can also use this filling to make phyllo triangles for an extra crispy treat!

HOT REUBEN DIP

SERVES 8 TO 10

INGREDIENTS

Cooking spray

12 ounces corned beef, chopped

8 ounces cream cheese, at room temperature

¼ cup sour cream

½ cup mayonnaise

3 tablespoons whole-grain mustard

1 cup shredded Swiss cheese

½ cup shredded Muenster cheese

¼ teaspoon caraway seed

¼ cup Thousand Island dressing

½ cup sauerkraut, drained

Cocktail rye bread or crackers for serving

DIRECTIONS

1 Spray an 8-inch baking dish pan with cooking spray.

2 In a bowl, stir together the corned beef, cream cheese, sour cream, mayonnaise, mustard, Swiss cheese, muenster cheese, and caraway seed. Spoon mixture into dish. Cook at 350°F for 12 to 15 minutes until cheese is melted and bubbly.

3 Remove dish from air fryer. Sprinkle sauerkraut over the dip and drizzle dressing on top. Serve with cocktail rye bread or crackers.

ERIC SAYS: Don't tell anyone, but you can use this mix for the best grilled cheese. Just put a good schmeer between two pieces of buttered rye. Cook at 400°F until the bread is a deep golden brown!

CREAMY EGGPLANT & ROASTED PEPPER DIP

MAKES ABOUT 2 CUPS

INGREDIENTS

1½ pounds eggplant, stemmed and halved lengthwise

1 red bell pepper, halved lengthwise, stemmed and seeded

Olive oil or olive oil cooking spray

2 cloves garlic, minced

2 tablespoons lemon juice

¼ teaspoon dried basil

¼ teaspoon dried oregano

1 (5.3-ounce) container plain Greek yogurt

½ cup crumbled feta cheese

½ teaspoon salt

4 pita breads, each cut into eighths

DIRECTIONS

1 Line the air fryer rack or bottom of air fryer basket with foil.

2 Poke the skin of each eggplant half a few times with a fork. Score the flesh diagonally with a knife. Brush flesh with olive oil or spray with olive oil spray. Place flesh-side down in the air fryer.

3 Cook at 400°F for 30 minutes. When flesh is soft and lightly charred, use tongs or an oven mitt to remove eggplant from air fryer. Set aside on a plate to cool.

4 Add the red pepper halves, flesh side down, to the air fryer. Cook at 400°F for 12 minutes. When pepper is softened and lightly charred, use tongs or an oven mitt to remove from the air fryer. Set aside with eggplant to cool.

5 When vegetables are cool enough to handle, remove the skin from both the eggplant and peppers and place in a food processor. Pulse a few times. Add the garlic, lemon juice, basil, oregano, yogurt, feta cheese, and salt. Pulse until desired texture. Transfer to a serving bowl.

6 Place the pita bread wedges in a single layer in the air fryer. Brush with olive oil or spray with olive oil spray. Cook at 325°F for 15 minutes, rotating the racks or tossing the basket every 5 minutes, until warmed and crisped.

7 Serve dip with pita wedges.

> **ERIC SAYS:** This dip is a blank canvas for any flavor profile. Add some pesto for Italian, gochjuang for Korean, or roasted green chilis and cumin for a Southwest flair.

ITALIAN PASTA CHIPS

SERVES 4 TO 6

INGREDIENTS

- 2 tablespoons olive oil
- 1 tablespoon balsamic vinegar
- 1 teaspoon onion powder
- ½ teaspoon garlic powder
- ½ teaspoon basil
- ½ teaspoon oregano
- ½ teaspoon each salt and pepper
- ½ cup grated Parmesan cheese
- ½ teaspoon red pepper flakes (optional)
- 8 ounces penne or rotini pasta, cooked according to package directions, drained
- Cooking spray
- 1 cup marinara sauce, warmed, for dipping

DIRECTIONS

1 In a large bowl, combine olive oil, vinegar, onion powder, garlic powder, basil, oregano, salt and pepper, Parmesan cheese,and red pepper flakes, if using. Add the pasta to the bowl and stir until well-coated.

2 Preheat air fryer to 400°F for 2 minutes. Spray air fryer shelves or basket with cooking spray. Add pasta to air fryer and cook for 10 to 12 minutes, stirring or shaking the basket every few minutes.

3 Pour pasta chips onto a large rimmed baking sheet to cool (they will continue to crisp up as they cool). Serve with warmed marinara sauce.

> **ERIC SAYS:** Think outside the box for these crispy treats. Add them to soups or salads instead of croutons or crackers.

SWEET & SOUR MEATBALLS

SERVES 6 TO 8

INGREDIENTS

FOR THE SWEET AND SOUR SAUCE

- 1 cup pineapple juice
- 1 tablespoon cornstarch
- ¼ cup white vinegar
- ½ cup ketchup
- 2 tablespoons brown sugar
- 1 cup crushed pineapple
- 1 teaspoon grated fresh ginger
- ¼ teaspoon red pepper flakes

FOR THE MEATBALLS

- 2 egg yolks, beaten
- 2 slices white bread, crusts removed, torn into small pieces
- ¼ cup milk
- ¼ cup grated onion
- ¼ teaspoon ground allspice
- 1 teaspoon salt
- ½ teaspoon pepper
- 1 teaspoon paprika
- ¼ teaspoon ground nutmeg
- ¾ pound ground beef
- ¾ pound ground pork
  Cooking spray

DIRECTIONS

1 For the sauce: In a small saucepan, whisk together pineapple juice and cornstarch. Add remaining sauce ingredients and bring to a simmer. Cook and stir until thickened. Remove from heat and set aside.

2 For the meatballs: In a bowl, combine egg yolks, bread, and milk. Add onion, allspice, salt, pepper, paprika, and nutmeg. Stir to combine. Add the beef and pork and mix until all ingredients are well incorporated. Form mixture into 1½-inch balls.

3 Preheat air fryer to 400°F. Spray air fryer shelves or basket with cooking spray. Place the meatballs in the air fryer. Reduce heat to 375°F and cook for 12 to 15 minutes or until browned and cooked through, turning halfway through the cooking time.

4 Serve with sweet and sour sauce.

> ERIC SAYS: Throw these meatballs on slider buns and top with pepper jack and crispy fried onions for an extra Hawaiian treat!

CRISPY BAJA SHRIMP

SERVES 4 TO 6

INGREDIENTS

FOR THE BAJA SAUCE

- ½ cup sour cream
- ½ cup mayonnaise
- ¼ cup chopped roasted green chilies, drained
- 2 tablespoons chopped fresh cilantro
- 1 teaspoon fresh lime juice

FOR THE SHRIMP

- 1 cup all-purpose flour
- 3 eggs, beaten
- 2 cups finely crushed Cool Ranch® Dorito® chips
- 1 pound large shrimp, peeled and deveined
- Cooking spray

DIRECTIONS

1 For the sauce: In a bowl, combine all ingredients. Stir until well blended and set aside.

2 For the shrimp: Place flour in a shallow bowl, eggs in another, and chips in a third. Lightly dust shrimp in flour. Dip in egg, then again in flour, and then in crushed chips.

3 Preheat air fryer at 400°F for 2 minutes. Spray air fryer shelves or basket with cooking spray. Place half of the shrimp in fryer and spray with cooking spray. Cook shrimp for 6 minutes or until crisp and cooked through, turning halfway through the cooking time. Repeat with remaining shrimp.

4 Serve immediately with Baja sauce.

> **ERIC SAYS:** Make sure to get individually frozen peeled and deveined shrimp to cut back on your prep time. These also make great tacos or lettuce wraps!

PARMESAN-BLACK PEPPER BISCOTTI

MAKES 12 TO 14

INGREDIENTS

2 tablespoons butter, room temperature

⅓ cup Parmesan cheese

3 tablespoons hot water

1 egg, beaten

1 cup all-purpose flour, plus more for dusting

1 teaspoon baking powder

1 teaspoon coarse-ground black pepper

1 teaspoon dried basil

½ teaspoon salt

Parchment paper

DIRECTIONS

1 In a small bowl, stir together the butter, cheese, and hot water until combined. Add egg and stir until combined.

2 In another bowl, combine the 1 cup flour, baking powder, black pepper, and basil. Add to the butter mixture and stir until a dough forms.

3 On a lightly floured surface, shape dough into an 8x4-inch rectangle.

4 Preheat air fryer at 325°F for 2 minutes.

5 Cut a piece of parchment to fit the air fryer rack or bottom of air fryer basket. Place dough on parchment paper and carefully place in air fryer. Cook at 325°F for 15 minutes. Remove and let cool until slightly warm.

6 When dough is cool enough to handle, carefully cut it into ½-inch slices with a serrated knife. Turn air fryer to 400°F. Place half of the slices in a single layer (without parchment paper) in air fryer. Cook for 15 minutes. Turn slices and cook for an additional 5 minutes. Repeat with remaining slices.

7 Cool on a wire rack (they will crisp up as they cool). Store in an air tight container until ready to serve.

> **ERIC SAYS:** I love to float one or two of these biscotti on top of bowl of creamy tomato soup.

FETA-WALNUT PUFFS WITH SPICED HONEY

MAKES 16 PUFFS

INGREDIENTS

½ cup walnut halves

4 ounces cream cheese, at room temperature

4 ounces crumbled feta cheese

All-purpose flour, for dusting

1 frozen puff pastry sheet, thawed

2 tablespoons honey

Pinch or two cayenne pepper, cinnamon, or both

DIRECTIONS

1 Place walnuts in a baking pan that fits the air fryer. Cook for 4 minutes at 375°F. Remove walnuts and let cool. When cool enough to handle, chop walnuts.

2 In a bowl, mix together the cream cheese, feta, and walnuts.

3 Lightly dust a work surface with flour. Unfold the puff pastry and roll out to an 11×11-inch square. Cut pastry into 16 squares. Place a tablespoon of filling in the middle of each square. Bring the corners of the puff pastry squares together to form a little purse and seal.

4 Place the puffs on an air fryer rack or basket and cook at 400°F for 12 minutes. When finished, let cool for 10 minutes.

5 While puffs are cooling, stir together the honey and the cayenne and/or cinnamon. Drizzle over the puffs before serving.

ERIC SAYS: These are absolutely delicious served hot with pistachio ice cream. It will add a nutty sweetness to contrast the tangy feta.

POTATO & CHEESE PUFFS

MAKES 20 PUFFS

INGREDIENTS

2 cups mashed potatoes

½ cup all-purpose flour, plus more if needed

1½ cups shredded Swiss cheese

2 egg yolks

1 teaspoon salt

¼ teaspoon pepper

1 cup panko breadcrumbs

Cooking spray

Truffle oil for finishing (optional)

DIRECTIONS

1 Line air fryer shelf or basket with parchment paper or foil.

2 In a bowl, stir together the mashed potatoes, the ½ cup flour, cheese, egg yolks, salt, and pepper. If mixture seems wet, add more flour to create a fairly firm consistency. Roll mixture into 1-inch balls and coat in breadcrumbs.

3 Preheat air fryer to 400°F for 2 minutes. Place puffs in air fryer. Spray with cooking spray. Cook for 10 minutes or until golden brown.

4 Cool 5 minutes before serving. Drizzle with truffle oil, if using.

> **ERIC SAYS:** Turn this into poutine by topping with cheese curds and a rich beef gravy!

"CHORIZO" STUFFED MUSHROOMS

SERVES 10 TO 12

INGREDIENTS

- 1 cup plant-based chorizo crumbles
- ½ cup finely diced red pepper
- ½ cup finely diced onion
- 2 tablespoons cream cheese, at room temperature
- 1 cup grated Cheddar cheese
- 1 pound large button mushrooms, stems removed
- Cooking spray

DIRECTIONS

1 In a small bowl, combine the chorizo, red pepper, onion, cream cheese, and Cheddar cheese. Stir until well combined. Fill each mushroom cap with about 1 tablespoon of the mixture. Spray mushrooms with cooking spray.

2 Arrange half of the mushrooms in the air fryer. Cook at 400°F for 8 minutes until cheese is melted and golden brown. Repeat with repmaining mushrooms. Serve warm.

> **ERIC SAYS:** I actually love to load these into a hoagie roll with sautéed spinach and melt provolone on top for a killer grinder.

FLAUTAS DE POLLO

MAKES 12

INGREDIENTS

FOR THE FLAUTAS

1 cup chopped cooked chicken

1 cup shredded Monterey Jack cheese

1 (15-ounce) can peeled white potatoes, drained and mashed with a fork

1 (1-ounce) package taco seasoning

12 corn tortillas

Cooking spray

FOR TOPPINGS (OPTIONAL)

Shredded lettuce

Salsa

Sour cream

Guacamole

Shredded cheese

Diced tomatoes

Chopped cilantro

DIRECTIONS

1 In a medium bowl, stir together the chicken, cheese, potatoes, and taco seasoning. Evenly divide filling among the tortillas. Roll up tortillas and close with a toothpick.

2 Place half of the flautas in the air fryer and spray with cooking spray. Cook at 400°F for 8 to 10 minutes or until crispy, turning halfway through the cooking time. Repeat with remaining flautas.

3 Serve with desired toppings.

> **ERIC SAYS:** I love to substitute the potatoes with sweet potatoes and add some caramelized onions and goat cheese for a different flavor profile!

TROPICAL BACON-WRAPPED SCALLOPS

MAKES 12

INGREDIENTS

FOR THE SCALLOPS

12 sea scallops

6 to 8 slices center-cut bacon, halved

12 toothpicks

1 tablespoon Jamaican jerk seasoning

Cooking spray

FOR THE CARIBBEAN SAUCE

¼ cup sweet chili sauce

¼ cup guava jelly

2 tablespoons fresh lime juice

DIRECTIONS

1 For the scallops: Pat scallops dry with a paper towel.

2 Wrap a half-strip of bacon around each scallop and close with a toothpick. Dust scallops with jerk seasoning.

3 Spray air fryer shelves or basket with cooking spray. Place the scallops in the air fryer and cook at 400°F for 8 to 10 minutes or until bacon is crispy, turning halfway through the cooking time.

4 For the sauce: While scallops are cooking, stir together sauce ingredients in a microwave-safe dish and heat for 30 seconds to warm. Glaze scallops with sauce.

ERIC SAYS: I love to substitute cubes of salmon for the scallops for a different take on this recipe!

NACHO CHEESE BALLS

MAKES 12 TO 14 BALLS

INGREDIENTS

4 ounces cream cheese, at room temperature

1½ cups shredded sharp Cheddar cheese

6 cups nacho cheese-flavored tortilla chips

¼ cup flour

2 eggs, beaten

Cooking spray

DIRECTIONS

1 In a bowl, stir together the cream cheese and Cheddar cheese and chill for at least 1 hour.

2 While mixture is chilling, place the tortilla chips in a food processor and process into semi-fine crumbs. Set aside.

3 Form chilled cheese mixture into 1 inch balls . Dredge cheese balls first in flour, dip in eggs, then coat them in tortilla chip crumbs. Dip again in eggs and then again in the tortilla chips. Set each coated ball on a tray or plate as you work. Freeze coated cheese balls for 10 minutes.

4 Place cheese balls in air fryer and spray with cooking spray. Cook at 390°F for 6 minutes. Cool for 5 minutes. Serve warm.

ERIC SAYS: Serve these with a creamy ranch dressing mixed with fresh salsa and a squeeze of fresh lime.

VEGGIES
FOR ALL

CAULIFLOWER STEAKS MILANESE

SERVES 2

INGREDIENTS

- 1 head cauliflower, leaves trimmed
- ¼ cup vinaigrette-style Caesar dressing
- 3 tablespoons mayonnaise
- ¼ cup panko breadcrumbs
- 2 tablespoons grated Parmesan cheese
- ½ teaspoon Italian seasoning
- ¼ teaspoon salt
- ⅛ teaspoon pepper
- Lemon wedges

DIRECTIONS

1 Trim the stem of the cauliflower, but leave it intact. Place cauliflower core-side down on a work surface. Using a large knife, cut the cauliflower in half through the center, then cut a 1½-inch slice from each half. Reserve outer loose cauliflower for another use.

2 Place the 2 cauliflower steaks on a plate and generously brush both sides with the Caesar dressing. Be sure to get the dressing in the nooks and crannies and on the sides. Let marinate for 5 to 10 minutes, then spread mayonnaise on one side of each steak.

3 Mix together the panko breadcrumbs, Parmesan cheese, Italian seasoning, salt, and pepper. Top each steak with the breadcrumb mixture, pressing it lightly into the mayonnaise.

4 Place steaks, breadcrumb side up, on air fryer rack or basket. Cook at 400°F for 20 minutes or until tender and breadcrumbs are browned.

5 Serve with lemon wedges.

> **ERIC SAYS:** Make it a *torta ahogada* by serving a red chili broth to dip the sandwich.

CAPRESE STUFFED PORTOBELLOS

SERVES 4

INGREDIENTS

- 2 tablespoons Dijon mustard
- ¼ cup + 2 tablespoons olive oil
- 4 tablespoons balsamic vinegar, divided
- 2 tablespoons honey
- 1 teaspoon Italian seasoning
- 2 cloves garlic, minced
- 1 teaspoon salt, divided
- ½ teaspoon pepper, divided
- 2 large portobello mushroom caps, washed, stem and gills removed
- 4 ounces fresh mozzarella, diced
- 1 cup cherry tomatoes, halved
- ¼ cup fresh basil leaves, torn

DIRECTIONS

1 In a bowl, combine the mustard, ¼ cup olive oil, 2 tablespoons of the balsamic vinegar, honey, Italian seasoning, ½ teaspoon salt, and ¼ teaspoon pepper.

2 Place the mushroom caps in a resealable storage bag and add the marinade. Let mushrooms marinate for 15 minutes.

3 Preheat air fryer at 400°F for 2 minutes. Remove the mushrooms from the marinade and place in air fryer. Cook mushrooms for 6 minutes, turning halfway through the cooking time.

4 In a bowl, combine the mozzarella, tomatoes, basil, remaining 2 tablespoons of balsamic, 2 tablespoons olive oil, ½ teaspoon salt, and ¼ teaspoon pepper. Mix well.

5 When the mushrooms are cooked, divide cheese mixture among the mushrooms. Cook mushrooms for an additional 4 to 6 more minutes, until cheese is melted.

ERIC SAYS: If I'm in the mood for something a little sharper, I will use Taleggio cheese. It's like an Italian brie and gets super creamy when it melts. Don't forget the garlicky greens!

PECAN-CRUSTED PORTOBELLO BURGERS WITH HONEY MUSTARD

SERVES 4

INGREDIENTS

1 cup pecans

½ teaspoon garlic powder

½ teaspoon salt

¼ teaspoon pepper

½ cup panko breadcrumbs

¼ cup all-purpose flour

2 eggs, beaten

4 large portobello mushroom caps, washed and dried, gills removed

4 hamburger buns

Lettuce

Sliced tomato

Sliced avocado

¼ cup honey mustard

¼ cup mayonnaise

DIRECTIONS

1 Place the pecans, garlic powder, salt, and pepper in a food processor. Pulse until the pecans are fine but still have some chunky pieces. Pour pecans into a shallow dish and add the panko crumbs. Mix together.

2 Set up a breading station by placing the flour and eggs in separate shallow dishes.

3 Dredge one of the mushrooms in the flour, then the egg. Press the pecan mixture onto the mushroom to form a crust. Repeat process with remaining mushrooms.

4 Place mushrooms in the air fryer. Cook at 380°F for 10 minutes, turning halfway through the cooking time.

5 While mushrooms are cooking, stir together the mustard and mayonnaise.

6 Top the bottom of each hamburger bun with lettuce, tomato, and avocado slices. Top with a mushroom and drizzle 2 tablespoons of the honey mustard sauce over each mushroom. Place bun top on mushroom.

ERIC SAYS: These burgers are almost like chicken-fried steak. Top with a cream gravy and serve with scrambled eggs for a Southern breakfast!

ROASTED BEET SALAD WITH BLUE CHEESE, ORANGES & PECANS

SERVES 4

INGREDIENTS

- 1 pound beets, peeled and cut into 1-inch pieces
- ¼ cup olive oil, divided
- Salt and pepper
- ½ cup chopped pecans
- 2 tablespoons balsamic vinegar
- 1 tablespoon honey
- 2 teaspoons Dijon mustard
- 1 clove garlic, minced
- ½ teaspoon Italian seasoning
- 8 cups salad greens or baby spinach
- 1 (11-ounce) can of mandarin oranges, drained
- 4 ounces crumbled blue cheese

DIRECTIONS

1 Toss the beets in 2 tablespoons of the olive oil and season with salt and pepper to taste. Place beets in air fryer. Cook at 400°F for 20 minutes, stirring or tossing beets halfway through cooking time. When tender, remove beets from air fryer and let cool.

2 Place pecans in a baking pan that fits air fryer. Toast at 375°F for 4 minutes. Remove pecans and let cool.

3 In a large bowl, whisk together the balsamic vinegar, honey, mustard, garlic, Italian seasoning and remaining 2 tablespoons of olive oil. Season with salt and pepper to taste. Add salad greens and beets to the bowl and toss with the dressing.

4 Divide salad among 4 bowls and top each salad with pecans, oranges, and blue cheese.

> **ERIC SAYS:** You can use any creamy sharp cheese like goat or feta. Pair with poached chicken for a bistro dish!

ROASTED CORN & BLACK BEAN SALAD

SERVES 4 TO 6

INGREDIENTS

3 ears of corn, shucked

2 tablespoons olive oil

Salt and pepper

1 (15.5 ounce) can of black beans, drained and rinsed

1 cup quartered cherry tomatoes

½ cup red pepper, diced

½ cup red onion, diced

¼ cup cilantro, chopped

½ jalapeño, stemmed, seeded and chopped fine

½ teaspoon chili powder

½ teaspoon cumin

2 cloves garlic, minced

¼ cup lime juice

¼ cup olive oil

Salt and pepper to taste

DIRECTIONS

1 Preheat air fryer for 2 minutes on 400°F.

2 Rub or spray the corn with oil. Season with salt and pepper. Place corn on air fryer rack or basket.

3 Cook at 400°F for 10 minutes, turning the corn halfway through cooking. When cooked, remove the corn and let cool.

4 When cooled enough to handle, cut the corn from the cob and place kernels in a large bowl. Add the black beans, cherry tomatoes, red pepper, onion, cilantro, jalapeño, chili powder, cumin, garlic, lime juice and olive oil to the corn. Toss together and season to taste.

5 Can be eaten alone or served with soft tortillas or chips.

ERIC SAYS: Mix with Monterey jack cheese, cream cheese, mayonnaise, then heat in a baking dish for an awesome hot dip!

SWEET POTATO SALAD

SERVES 8 TO 10

INGREDIENTS

2 pounds sweet potatoes, peeled and cut into ½-inch dice

1½ teaspoons salt, divided

¼ teaspoon pepper

2 tablespoons vegetable oil

½ cup mayonnaise

2 tablespoons lime juice

1 cup cilantro leaves, finely chopped

¼ teaspoon garlic powder

¼ teaspoon smoked paprika

Hot sauce

½ red bell pepper, diced

½ green bell pepper, diced

½ cup finely diced sweet onion

DIRECTIONS

1 Place potatoes in a large bowl and toss with 1 teaspoon salt, pepper, and oil.

2 Preheat air fryer to 380°F degrees for 2 minutes. Place potatoes in a single layer on two air fryer racks or in fryer basket. (Cook in batches if necessary). Cook for 20 minutes, rotating racks or tossing basket halfway through the cooking time, until potatoes are tender but not mushy.

3 While potatoes are cooking, in a large bowl, combine the mayonnaise, lime juice, cilantro, garlic powder, paprika, remaining salt, and hot sauce to taste.

4 When potatoes are finished cooking, let cool completely. Add potatoes, red and green peppers, and onion to bowl and toss gently until everything is combined and well-coated with the dressing.

5 Cover and chill until serving time.

SAVORY ZUCCHINI-GOAT CHEESE TART

SERVES 4 TO 6

INGREDIENTS

- ½ cup ricotta cheese
- 1 tablespoon lemon zest
- Salt and pepper
- 2 ounces goat cheese crumbles
- 1 (9-inch) refrigerated pie crust, at room temperature
- 2 small zucchini, sliced into ¼-inch rounds
- Cooking spray
- 1 teaspoon dried basil
- 2 tablespoons marinara sauce
- 1 tablespoon grated Parmesan cheese

DIRECTIONS

1 Mix the ricotta with lemon zest and salt and pepper to taste. Fold in the goat cheese.

2 Unroll pie crust on a small baking sheet. Spread the cheese mixture over the center of the crust, leaving a 1-inch border bare. Shingle the zucchini, in a circle, on the cheese. Spray with cooking spray. Season with the basil and salt and pepper to taste. Dollop the marinara over the zucchini and sprinkle with Parmesan.

3 Fold in the bare edges of the crust toward the center. Place the tart in the air fryer and cook at 390°F for 10 to 12 minutes.

4 Remove tart from air fryer and let cool for 10 minutes before serving.

ERIC SAYS: This works best in an oven-style air fryer. You can also make this the day before and serve at room temperature if you are going to prep for a party. I also serve this with a creamy yogurt dill sauce.

EGGPLANT "MEATBALLS"

MAKES 20

INGREDIENTS

- 1 small eggplant, stemmed and halved lengthwise
- 1 clove garlic
- ¼ cup chopped onion
- ¼ cup walnuts
- 4 slices white bread, torn
- 2 tablespoons Parmesan cheese
- 1 tablespoon lemon juice
- ½ teaspoon dried basil
- ½ teaspoon dried oregano
- ½ teaspoon salt
- ½ teaspoon cumin
- ¼ teaspoon pepper
- 1 (14-ounce) can lentils, drained and rinsed (or 1½ cups cooked lentils)
- 1 egg
- Warm marinara for serving

DIRECTIONS

1 Score the flesh of the eggplant with a knife and pierce the skin a few times with a fork. Place eggplant halves on an air fryer rack or in air fryer basket.

2 Cook at 400°F for 20 minutes. When flesh is soft, use tongs to remove eggplant from air fryer. Set aside on a plate to cool. When cool enough to handle, remove the skin from the eggplant, then chop into large pieces.

3 In the bowl of a food processor combine the garlic, onion, walnuts, bread, Parmesan cheese, lemon juice, basil, oregano, salt, cumin, and pepper. Pulse until mixture looks like breadcrumbs. Add the chopped eggplant, lentils, and egg to the crumbs. Pulse until combined and resembles "meatball" mix. There may be some small chunks of eggplant or nuts—that is fine.

4 Form 1-tablespoon portions of the mixture into round balls. Line an air fryer rack or air fryer basket with foil and spray with cooking spray. Preheat air fryer at 370°F for 2 minutes.

5 Working in batches, place the "meatballs" in a single, uncrowded layer on the foil. Cook for 10 minutes at 370°F.

6 Serve with warm marinara.

> **ERIC SAYS:** I love these meatballs on a crusty ciabatta roll with fresh mozzarella, pesto, and baby arugula to make a trattoria dish.

PARMESAN TRUFFLE FRIES WITH HOT BRUSCHETTA DIP

pictured on back cover

SERVES 2 TO 3

INGREDIENTS

FOR THE FRIES

- 2 medium Yukon gold potatoes, scrubbed and peeled (if desired)
- 1 tablespoon olive oil
- ½ teaspoon salt
- ¼ teaspoon black pepper
- ½ cup grated Parmesan cheese
- ¼ cup chopped Italian parsley
- Truffle oil for drizzling

FOR THE DIP

- 2 tablespoons olive oil
- 2 pints cherry or grape tomatoes
- ¼ cup chopped red onion
- ½ teaspoon red chili flakes
- Salt and pepper
- 3 tablespoons cream cheese
- 1 teaspoon tomato paste
- 6 basil leaves
- 3 garlic cloves, crushed and peeled
- Bottled balsamic reduction, for garnish

DIRECTIONS

1 Make the fries: Cut the potatoes into ¼-inch-thick planks. Submerge in a bowl of cold water and let soak for 20 minutes. Preheat air fryer to 375°F.

2 Drain potatoes and pat dry with a paper towel. Dry the bowl and place fries back in bowl. Drizzle with the olive oil and season with the salt and pepper.

3 Arrange fries in a single layer on the air fryer rack or in basket and cook for 10 or 15 minutes or until crispy and golden brown, shaking every 5 minutes to ensure even cooking.

4 While the fries are cooking, make the dip: Heat the oil in a medium pot over medium-high heat. Add the tomatoes and cook, stirring occasionally, until tomato skins begin to sear and brown. Add the red onion and chili flakes. Season to taste with salt and pepper. Cook, stirring occasionally, mashing tomatoes to release their juices, until onions are tender. Remove 1 tablespoon of the tomato mixture and set aside.

5 Add the cream cheese, tomato paste, 4 of the basil leaves, and garlic. Cook and stir until well blended. Turn heat to low and simmer until garlic is tender, about 10 minutes.

6 Remove the basil leaves from mixture and discard. Pour mixture into a blender or use an immersion blender and blend until smooth. Transfer to a bowl. Top with reserved tomato mixture. Drizzle with balsamic reduction and garnish with remaining 2 basil leaves.

7 Remove fries from air fryer and toss immediately with Parmesan cheese and chopped parsley. Drizzle lightly with truffle oil. Serve with hot bruschetta dip.

LEMONY BEANS & GREENS ON TOAST

SERVES 4

INGREDIENTS

- 4 slices frozen Texas toast garlic bread
- 1 (15-ounce) can cannellini beans, rinsed and drained
- Zest of 1 lemon
- 2 tablespoons lemon juice, divided
- 2 tablespoons olive oil, divided
- 2 tablespoons grated Parmesan cheese
- ¼ teaspoon crushed red pepper
- 1 clove garlic, minced
- ½ teaspoon salt
- 2 cups frozen chopped kale or spinach, defrosted and squeezed dry
- 4 slices provolone cheese

DIRECTIONS

1 Preheat air fryer at 400°F for 2 minutes, then place the garlic bread in air fryer. Toast bread for 4 minutes or until very lightly toasted, turning halfway through the cooking time. When cooked, remove toast from air fryer and set on a plate.

2 In a bowl, mash together the cannellini beans, lemon zest, 1 tablespoon of the lemon juice, 1 tablespoon of the olive oil, Parmesan cheese, crushed red pepper, and salt.

3 In another bowl combine the kale or spinach greens with the remaining lemon juice and olive oil.

4 Spread an equal amount of the bean mixture on each piece of toast. Top with the beans greens and place a slice of provolone on top.

5 Place the toast in the air fryer and cook, in batches if necessary, at 400°F for 4 to 5 minutes or until cheese is melted and golden brown.

SCALLION PANCAKES

MAKES 4

INGREDIENTS

FOR THE DIPPING SAUCE

- ⅓ cup soy sauce
- 1 tablespoon grated fresh ginger
- 1 tablespoon rice wine vinegar
- 1 tablespoon brown sugar
- 2 teaspoons sesame oil
- 1 scallion, sliced

FOR THE PANCAKES

- 1 cup flour
- ¼ teaspoon salt
- ⅓ cup hot water
- 2 tablespoons sesame oil
- 3 scallions, thinly sliced
- 3 tablespoons vegetable oil

DIRECTIONS

1 For the sauce: Combine the soy sauce, ginger, rice wine vinegar, brown sugar, sesame oil ,and scallions in a bowl. Set aside to serve with pancakes.

2 For the pancakes: Combine flour, salt, and water in bowl and knead together until a dough that is pliable but not sticky forms, adding flour or water as necessary. Form dough into a ball and cover with a damp towel. Let rest for 30 minutes.

3 Cut dough into 4 pieces and form into balls. On a lightly floured surface, roll a ball of dough into a thin 8-inch round. Brush surface with sesame oil. Sprinkle one-fourth of the scallions over the pancake.

4 Roll the pancake into a cigar-shaped cylinder. Shape the cylinder into a coil and then flatten with your hand. Roll out again into a 7-inch round. Repeat with 3 other dough balls.

5 Preheat air fryer at 400°F for 5 minutes. Brush one side of a pancake with vegetable oil. Place the pancake, oil side down, on an air fryer rack or into the basket. Brush the top of the pancake with vegetable oil.

6 Cook for 4 minutes. Turn and cook for an additional 4 minutes. Repeat with 3 other pancakes.

7 Cut each pancake into 4 wedges and serve with dipping sauce.

> **ERIC SAYS:** I love to top the pancake wedges with some thinly sliced sushi-grade tuna or smoked salmon and turn these into little canapes!

FOLD IT, ROLL IT
TOSS IT

PIZZA, CALZONES, AND STROMBOLI

POLYNESIAN BBQ SHRIMP PIZZA

SERVES 2

INGREDIENTS

- ¼ cup sweet chili sauce
- 2 prebaked (8-inch) pizza crusts
- 1 cup shredded mozzarella
- 1 tablespoon hoisin sauce
- 1 tablespoon barbecue sauce
- ¼ teaspoon curry powder
- 1 cup cooked shrimp, chopped
- ½ cup chopped pineapple
- 2 tablespoons chopped scallions
- 2 tablespoons toasted coconut
- Cooking spray

DIRECTIONS

1 Spread sweet chili sauce on the crusts, then top with mozzarella cheese.

2 In a bowl, stir together the hoisin sauce, barbecue sauce, and curry powder. Add shrimp and toss to coat. Divide between crusts. Top with pineapple, scallions, and coconut.

3 Spray air fryer shelves or basket with cooking spray. If using an oven-style fryer, place both crusts in air fryer. If using a basket style fryer, cook one pizza at a time.

4 Cook pizza at 350°F for 10 minutes or until cheese is golden brown, rotating shelves halfway through the cooking time if you are using an oven-style fryer.

> **ERIC SAYS:** I love to add unusual textures to my pizza. Topping with crispy fried wontons after cooking is a great twist!

CHICKEN FUNDIDO CALZONE

MAKES 2

INGREDIENTS

   All-purpose flour, for dusting

1 (11-ounce) can refrigerated thin-crust pizza dough

1 cup cooked shredded chicken

¼ cup diced Hatch green chiles

¼ cup chopped roasted red peppers

1 cup shredded mozzarella

1 cup diced Velveeta

¼ teaspoon cumin

¼ teaspoon garlic powder

   Cooking spray

DIRECTIONS

1 Unroll pizza dough on a lightly floured surface and cut in half across the short length.

2 In a bowl, combine chicken, green chiles, red peppers, mozzarella, Velveeta, cumin, and garlic powder. Mix well. Divide filling between dough pieces, placing it on one half of each crust and leaving a ½-inch border.

3 Fold dough over filling and use a fork to seal the edges to form a rectangular-shaped pastry. Make 2 small air vents in each calzone with a paring knife.

4 Spray air fryer racks or basket with cooking spray. Place each calzone on a rack or in the basket. Cook at 400°F for 15 minutes, rotating halfway through the cooking time, or until calzone is golden brown.

> **ERIC SAYS:** Traditional queso fundido usually has spicy chorizo sausage, so adding it into the calzone will add a Latin flair!

CHICKEN, SPINACH & ARTICHOKE CALZONE

MAKES 2

INGREDIENTS

All-purpose flour, for dusting

1 (11-ounce) can refrigerated thin-crust pizza dough

½ cup ricotta cheese

1 cup shredded cooked chicken

¼ cup chopped frozen spinach, squeezed dry

½ cup marinated artichoke hearts, drained and chopped

1 cup shredded mozzarella

¼ cup grated Parmesan cheese

Cooking spray

DIRECTIONS

1 Lightly flour a work surface. Unroll pizza dough and cut in half across the short length. Divide the ricotta cheese between dough pieces, placing it on one half of each crust and leaving a ½-inch border. Top with chicken, spinach, artichokes, mozzarella , and Parmesan.

2 Fold dough over filling and use a fork to seal the edges to form a rectangular-shaped pastry. Make 2 small air vents in each calzone with a paring knife.

3 Spray air fryer racks or basket with cooking spray. Place each calzone on a rack or in the basket. Cook at 400°F for 15 minutes, rotating halfway through the cooking time, or until calzone is golden brown.

> **ERIC SAYS:** When the calzone are hot out of the air fryer, give them a brush of fresh garlic butter and a sprinkle of grated Parmesan cheese to take them over the top!

BUFFALO CAULIFLOWER PIZZA

MAKES 2

INGREDIENTS

- ½ cup Alfredo sauce
- 2 prebaked (8-inch) pizza crusts
- 1 cup shredded mozzarella
- ½ cup shredded Cheddar
- 1 (13-ounce) bag buffalo cauliflower, cooked for half of the time on the package directions
- ½ cup chopped celery
- ¼ cup chopped carrot
- ¼ cup crumbled blue cheese
- Cooking spray
- Buffalo sauce

DIRECTIONS

1 Spread Alfredo sauce on the crusts. Top with mozzarella cheese Cheddar, cauliflower, celery, carrots, and blue cheese.

2 Spray air fryer shelves or basket with cooking spray. If using an oven-style fryer, place both crusts in air fryer. If using a basket style fryer, cook one pizza at a time.

3 Cook pizza at 350°F for 10 minutes or until cheese is golden brown, rotating shelves halfway through the cooking time if you are using an oven-style fryer.

4 Drizzle with buffalo sauce.

> **ERIC SAYS:** If you want to get a true Buffalo chicken flavor, you can use cooked chicken nuggets or breaded tenders. Just give them a quick chop.

QUATTRO FUNGHI CALZONE

MAKES 2

INGREDIENTS

All-purpose flour

1 (11-ounce) can refrigerated thin-crust pizza dough

1 teaspoon truffle oil

½ cup ricotta cheese

¼ teaspoon pepper

½ cup each chopped sautéed portobello, cremini, oyster, and shiitake mushrooms

½ cup shredded mozzarella cheese

½ cup shredded fontina cheese

½ teaspoon chopped fresh thyme

Cooking spray

DIRECTIONS

1 Lightly flour a work surface. Unroll pizza dough and cut in half across the short length. Brush truffle oil on each crust. Divide the ricotta cheese between dough pieces, placing it on one half of each crust and leaving a ½-inch border. Sprinkle with pepper.

2 Top with mushrooms, mozzarella cheese, fontina cheese and thyme.

3 Fold dough over filling and use a fork to seal the edges to form a rectangular-shaped pastry. Make 2 small air vents in each calzone with a paring knife.

4 Spray air fryer racks or basket with cooking spray. Place each calzone on a rack or in the basket. Cook at 400°F for 15 minutes, rotating halfway through the cooking time, or until calzone is golden brown.

> **ERIC SAYS:** Dried porcini mushrooms are one of my favorite ingredients. Rehydrate in a little warm water and add to the mushroom mix for that intense umami flavor.

DETROIT-STYLE BURGER PIZZA

MAKES 2

INGREDIENTS

Cooking spray

1 (13-ounce) can refrigerated classic pizza crust dough

½ cup Thousand Island dressing

2 cups shredded mozzarella cheese

1 cup shredded yellow Cheddar cheese

1 cup cooked ground beef

1 cup sautéed chopped onions

2 cups shredded lettuce

1 cup chopped tomato

½ cup chopped dill pickles

DIRECTIONS

1 Spray two 8-inch square pans with cooking spray. (Use 8-inch rounds pans if using a basket-style fryer.) Cut dough in half and press into pans. Cover and let rise at room temperature for 1 hour.

2 Place pans on shelves in fryer. (If you have a basket-style fryer, work with one pan at a time.) Cook at 300°F for 7 to 10 minutes or until light brown. Allow crusts to cool.

3 Spread dressing on cooled crusts. Top with the mozzarella and Cheddar cheeses, pushing the cheese to the edges of the pans. Divide ground beef and onions between pans.

4 Cook pizza at 350°F for 10 minutes or until cheese is golden brown, rotating shelves halfway through the cooking time if you are using an oven-style fryer.

5 Top with lettuce, tomato, and pickles.

> **ERIC SAYS:** You can also use plant-based meat as a substitute for the beef and still get that delicious burger flavor.

CLAMS CASINO PIZZA

MAKES 2

INGREDIENTS

- ½ cup Alfredo sauce, plus more for dipping
- 1 clove garlic, minced
- 2 prebaked (8-inch) pizza crusts
- 1 cup shredded mozzarella
- ½ cup cooked chopped clams
- ¼ cup chopped green pepper
- ¼ cup chopped onion
- ½ cup crumbled crisp-cooked bacon
- ½ cup grated Parmesan cheese
- ¼ cup Italian seasoned breadcrumbs
- Cooking spray

DIRECTIONS

1 Stir together the ½ cup Alfredo sauce and garlic. Spread sauce on the crusts, then top with mozzarella, clams, green pepper, onion, bacon, and Parmesan cheese. Sprinkle breadcrumbs on top.

2 Spray air fryer shelves or basket with cooking spray. If using an oven-style fryer, place both crusts in air fryer. If using a basket style fryer, cook one pizza at a time.

3 Cook pizza at 350°F for 10 minutes or until cheese is golden brown, rotating shelves halfway through the cooking time if you are using an oven-style fryer.

4 Serve with Alfredo sauce for dipping.

ERIC SAYS: You can make a Manhattan-style clams casino pizza by using tomato sauce instead of the Alfredo sauce.

FARMER SOLSTICE CALZONE

MAKES 2

INGREDIENTS

All-purpose flour

1 (11-ounce) can refrigerated thin-crust pizza dough

½ cup ricotta cheese

½ cup shredded mozzarella cheese

½ cup shredded smoked Gouda cheese

1 cup cooked diced sweet potato

½ cup sautéed chopped kale

½ cup sautéed cremini mushrooms

¼ cup toasted pine nuts

¼ cup dried cranberries

Cooking spray

Horseradish sauce for dipping (optional)

DIRECTIONS

1 Lightly flour a work surface. Unroll pizza dough and cut in half across the short length. Divide the ricotta cheese between dough pieces, placing it on one half of each crust and leaving a ½-inch border. Top with mozzarella, Gouda, sweet potato, kale, mushrooms, pine nuts, and dried cranberries.

2 Fold dough over filling and use a fork to seal the edges to form a rectangular-shaped pastry. Make 2 small air vents in each calzone with a paring knife.

3 Spray air fryer racks or basket with cooking spray. Place each calzone on a rack or in the basket. Cook at 400°F for 15 minutes, rotating halfway through the cooking time, or until calzone is golden brown.

4 Serve with horseradish sauce, if using.

> **ERIC SAYS:** The beauty, and purpose of this pizza is to use farm- fresh seasonal vegetables. Just make sure you sauté and cool first, or all the moisture from the vegetables will water down the calzone.

FIG & GOAT CHEESE PIZZA

MAKES 2

INGREDIENTS

- 2 prebaked (8-inch) pizza crusts
- 1 tablespoon olive oil
- 1 cup baby arugula
- 1 cup shredded mozzarella cheese
- ½ cup chopped dried figs
- ½ cup crispy bacon
- ½ cup crumbled goat cheese
- Cooking spray

DIRECTIONS

1 Brush crusts with the olive oil. Top with arugula, mozzarella, figs, bacon, and goat cheese.

2 Spray air fryer shelves or basket with cooking spray. If using an oven-style fryer, place both crusts in air fryer. If using a basket style fryer, cook one pizza at a time.

3 Cook pizza at 350°F for 10 minutes or until cheese is golden brown, rotating shelves halfway through the cooking time if you are using an oven-style fryer.

> **ERIC SAYS:** I'm a big fan of adding some shaved peppered ham on top of this pizza after it comes out of the air fryer! Don't forget a little drizzle of aged balsamic vinegar.

POLKA STROMBOLI

MAKES 2

INGREDIENTS

All-purpose flour

1 (11-ounce) can refrigerated thin-crust pizza dough

¼ cup spicy brown mustard

1 cup chopped kielbasa

½ cup sautéed onions

½ cup sautéed green peppers

½ cup shredded mozzarella

½ cup shredded muenster cheese

½ teaspoon paprika

¼ teaspoon caraway seed

Cooking spray

DIRECTIONS

1 Lightly flour a work surface. Unroll pizza dough and cut in half across the short length. Spread mustard over each piece of dough, leaving a ½-inch border. Top with kielbasa, onions, green peppers, mozzarella, and muenster cheese. Sprinkle with paprika and caraway.

2 Starting at a short end, carefully roll dough over filling to create a spiraled roll.

3 Spray air fryer racks or basket with cooking spray. Place each stromboli on a rack. Cook at 400°F for 15 minutes, rotating halfway through cooking, until stromboli is golden brown. (Cook one stromboli at a time if using a basket-style fryer).

4 Let stand 5 minutes, then cut into 2- or 3-inch pieces to serve.

> **ERIC SAYS:** Serving the stromboli with a sour cream and paprika sauce will complete this polka party!

SPICY CHICAGO BEEF STROMBOLI

MAKES 2

INGREDIENTS

   All-purpose flour
1 (11-ounce) can refrigerated thin-crust pizza dough
1 cup chopped roast beef
¼ cup giardinera, coarsely chopped
¼ cup chopped roasted red peppers
¼ cup grated Parmesan cheese
1 cup shredded mozzarella
½ teaspoon dried oregano
¼ teaspoon garlic powder
¼ teaspoon red chili flakes
   Cooking spray

DIRECTIONS

1 Lightly flour a work surface. Unroll pizza dough and cut in half across the short length. Top each piece of dough with roast beef, giardinera, red peppers, Parmesan, and mozzarella cheese, leaving a ½-inch border. Sprinkle with oregano, red chili flakes, and garlic powder.

3 Starting at a short end, carefully roll dough over filling to create a spiraled roll.

4 Spray air fryer racks or basket with cooking spray. Place each stromboli on a rack. Cook at 400°F for 15 minutes, rotating halfway through cooking, until stromboli is golden brown. (Cook one stromboli at a time if using a basket-style fryer).

5 Let stand 5 minutes, then cut into 2- or 3-inch pieces to serve.

> **ERIC SAYS:** Everyone loves to dip their pizza in sauce. A creamy horseradish sauce goes great with the beef!

MONTE CRISTO FLATBREAD MELTS

SERVES 4

INGREDIENTS

- All-purpose flour
- 1 (11-ounce) can refrigerated pizza dough
- Cooking spray
- 2 tablespoons seedless raspberry jam
- 1 tablespoon mayonnaise
- 1 tablespoon Dijon mustard
- 8 slices deli ham
- 8 slices deli turkey
- 4 slices Swiss cheese
- Powdered sugar for dusting

DIRECTIONS

1 Lightly flour a work surface. Unroll pizza dough and cut in half across the short length.

2 Spray the racks or basket of air fryer with cooking spray. Preheat fryer at 400°F for 2 minutes. Carefully lay one of the dough pieces on rack or in the basket. Cook for 5 minutes. Repeat with second piece of dough.

3 Spread 1 tablespoon of the jam on one half of the lightly browned piece of dough. Spread half each of the mayonnaise and mustard on the opposite end of the same piece of dough. Repeat with second piece of dough.

4 Lay 4 slices each of the of ham and turkey and 2 slices of cheese on top of the jam on each piece of dough. Fold the mayonnaise-mustard side over the meat and cheese, forming an envelope fold.

5 If using an oven-style fryer, place both flatbreads on the racks of the fryer. If using a basket-style fryer, work with one flatbread at a time. Cook at 400°F for 10 minutes, flipping the flatbreads halfway through the cooking time.

6 Let cool for 5 minutes. When ready to serve, cut flatbreads in half and dust with powdered sugar.

> **ERIC SAYS:** You can turn this into a delicious brunch dish by topping with 2 perfectly poached eggs!

YOU HAD ME AT
CHICKEN

KOREAN STICKY DRUMSTICKS

MAKES 6 TO 8

INGREDIENTS

- 3 tablespoons Korean gochujang sauce
- 2 tablespoons grated fresh ginger
- 1 tablespoon minced garlic
- 1 tablespoon toasted sesame oil
- 1 tablespoon rice wine vinegar
- 1 tablespoon soy sauce
- 3 tablespoons brown sugar
- 1 teaspoon fish sauce
- 1 tablespoon mirin rice wine
- 1 tablespoon white miso
- 6 to 8 chicken drumsticks
- Cooking spray
- 1 tablespoon sesame seeds, toasted
- ½ cup chopped scallions

DIRECTIONS

1 In a large bowl, combine gochujang, ginger, garlic, sesame oil, vinegar, soy sauce, brown sugar, fish sauce, rice wine, and miso. Mix well and reserve about one-third of the sauce.

2 Add drumsticks to remaining marinade in bowl and toss to coat. Cover and marinate in the refrigerator for at least 30 minutes.

3 Spray air fryer shelves or basket with cooking spray and arrange chicken in fryer. Cook at 375°F for 10 minutes. Turn drumsticks and baste with sauce in which they marinated. Increase temperature to 400°F and cook for another 5 to 7 minutes or until skin is brown and crispy.

4 Arrange drumsticks on a plate or platter. Baste with reserved sauce, then sprinkle with sesame seeds and chopped scallions.

> **ERIC SAYS:** I love to serve these with a coconut sticky rice and pickled vegetable or kimchee. This chicken is fantastic cold the next day for lunch!

STUFFED CHICKEN FLORENTINE

SERVES 4

INGREDIENTS

- 4 ounces cream cheese, softened
- ¼ cup chopped crisp-cooked bacon
- ¼ cup grated Parmesan cheese
- 2 tablespoons mayonnaise
- 1½ cups chopped baby spinach
- 4 boneless, skinless chicken breasts
- Cooking spray

DIRECTIONS

1 In a bowl, combine cream cheese, bacon, Parmesan cheese, mayonnaise and spinach.

2 Place the chicken breasts on a cutting board and use a sharp knife to cut a pocket into the side of each chicken breast. Stuff each breast with the spinach mixture.

3 Spray air fryer shelves or basket with cooking spray and arrange chicken in fryer. Cook at 375°F for about 20 to 25 minutes or until meat reaches an internal temperature of 165°F.

KETO FRIED CHICKEN TENDERS

SERVES 4

INGREDIENTS

- 3 cups finely ground pork rinds
- ½ cup grated Parmesan cheese
- 1 teaspoon garlic powder
- ½ teaspoon paprika
- ½ teaspoon cumin
- ½ teaspoon ground turmeric
- 1 cup almond flour
- 4 eggs
- 1 cup heavy cream
- 1 pound chicken tenderloins
- Cooking spray

DIRECTIONS

1 In a medium-size bowl, combine pork rinds, cheese, garlic powder, paprika, cumin, and turmeric. Place almond flour in a second bowl. In a third bowl, beat eggs and cream together.

2 Dip chicken in the almond flour, coating all sides, then dip into the egg mixture, allowing excess to drip back into the bowl, then dip into the pork rind mixture. Place on a baking sheet. Repeat dipping process with all chicken pieces. Refrigerate chicken for 15 minutes.

3 Spray air fryer racks or basket with cooking spray. Cook chicken, in batches if necessary, at 375°F for about 25 to 30 min or until golden brown and meat has reached an internal temperature of 165°F.

KETO FRIED CHICKEN FLORENTINE

SERVES 4

INGREDIENTS

4 boneless, skinless chicken breasts

2 tablespoons butter, softened

1 teaspoon Italian seasoning

1½ cups frozen chopped spinach, thawed and squeezed dry

4 ounces cream cheese, softened

1 cup grated Parmesan cheese, divided

1 teaspoon chopped garlic

1 teaspoon salt

1 teaspoon pepper

8 slices bacon

2 large eggs

½ cup whole milk

½ cup almond flour

¾ cup finely ground pork rinds

½ teaspoon garlic powder

1 teaspoon dried oregano

Cooking spray

DIRECTIONS

1 Flatten chicken breasts to ⅛-inch thickness with a meat mallet. Spread butter on one side of the chicken, then sprinkle with Italian seasoning.

2 In a small bowl, combine spinach, cream cheese, ½ cup of the Parmesan cheese, garlic, salt, and pepper. Spread mixture over breasts, leaving a ½-inch border. Tightly roll up breasts. Wrap each roll with 2 slices of bacon and secure with toothpicks.

3 In a small bowl, beat eggs and milk together. Place almond flour in a shallow dish. In a second shallow dish, combine the pork rinds, garlic powder, oregano, and remaining ½ cup Parmesan cheese. Mix well.

4 Dip each chicken breast in the egg mixture, then in the almond flour. Dip again in egg mixture, then coat with pork rind mixture.

5 Spray air fryer rack or basket with cooking spray and place chicken in fryer. Cook at 350°F for 25 minutes or until golden brown and the meat reaches an internal temperature of 165°F.

CARIBBEAN CHICKEN SALAD SLIDERS

MAKES 12 TO 16

INGREDIENTS

2 (4 pound) whole chickens

½ cup bottled Jamaican jerk marinade

Cooking spray

¼ cup chopped celery

¼ cup chopped scallions

¼ cup chopped cucumber

¼ cup golden raisins

¼ cup chopped fresh pineapple

3 tablespoons chopped fresh cilantro

2 tablespoons fresh lime juice

1 teaspoon Jamaican jerk seasoning

¼ teaspoon curry powder

¾ cup mayonnaise

Sweet roll slider buns

DIRECTIONS

1 Place a chicken on the cutting board, breast side down. Use kitchen shears to cut out spine on each side. Press flat. Repeat with other chicken. Rub marinade over chickens, then marinate for at least 30 minutes in the refrigerator.

2 Spray air fryer shelves or basket with cooking spray and place one chicken skin side down in the fryer. Cook at 350°F for 20 minutes. Using tongs, flip the chicken over and continue cooking for another 15 minutes or until meat reaches an internal temperature of 165°F degrees. Repeat with other chicken. Let chickens cool until cool enough to handle. Pick all of the meat off and place in a large mixing bowl.

3 Add celery, scallions, cucumber, raisins, pineapple, cilantro, lime juice, jerk seasoning, curry powder, and mayonnaise to chicken. Stir well to combine. Refrigerate until ready to serve.

4 Serve on sweet roll slider buns.

> **ERIC SAYS:** I've made a delicious chicken pasta salad by tossing in some cooked penne pasta and adding a little more mayo to smooth it out.

CHICKEN SHAWARMA SANDWICHES

MAKES 4 TO 6

INGREDIENTS

FOR THE CHICKEN

- 3 tablespoons lemon juice
- 2 tablespoons chopped garlic
- ½ teaspoon ground cumin
- ½ teaspoon ground coriander
- 1 teaspoon smoked paprika
- ¼ teaspoon turmeric
- ¼ teaspoon ground allspice
- ½ teaspoon salt
- 1 teaspoon pepper
- 1 pound boneless, skinless chicken thighs
- Cooking spray

FOR THE SAUCE

- ½ cup plain Greek yogurt
- 1 tablespoon chopped fresh mint
- 1 tablespoon lemon juice
- ½ cup chopped seedless cucumber
- ¼ cup chopped red onion

FOR SERVING

- 4 to 6 fresh croissants
- Baby arugula
- Fresh tomato, sliced

DIRECTIONS

1 For the chicken: In a large bowl, mix lemon juice, garlic, cumin, coriander, paprika, turmeric, allspice, salt, and pepper. Add chicken and toss to coat. Cover and marinate in the refrigerator for at least 30 minutes.

2 For the sauce: In a small bowl, mix Greek yogurt, mint, lemon juice, cucumber, and red onion. Set aside.

3 Spray air fryer shelves or basket with cooking spray and arrange chicken in fryer. Cook at 400°F for about 12 to 15 minutes or until cooked through. Remove chicken from fryer. Let rest 5 to 10 minutes, then slice.

4 To serve: Slice croissants in half horizontally. Top bottom half with arugula, tomato, and chicken. Top with sauce.

> **ERIC SAYS:** I love to turn this sandwich into a bowl by swapping out the croissant for healthy grains. Farro is an ancient wheat grain and is one of my favorites. Couscous or a turmeric rice would be delicious as well.

SPICY SPATCHCOCK CHICKEN

SERVES 3 TO 4

INGREDIENTS

FOR THE CHICKEN

- ½ cup mayonnaise
- 2 tablespoons crushed sea salt
- 2 tablespoons smoked paprika
- 1 teaspoon sugar
- 1 tablespoon turmeric
- 2 teaspoons garlic powder
- 2 teaspoons granulated dried onion
- 1 tablespoon ground thyme
- 1 teaspoon mustard powder
- ½ teaspoon cayenne pepper
- 2 teaspoons dried lemon peel
- 1 tablespoon ground black pepper
- 2 tablespoons olive oil
- 1 (4-pound) whole chicken, spine and breastbone removed

FOR THE LOUISIANA HOT SAUCE

- ½ cup butter
- 2 tablespoons brown sugar
- 2 teaspoons kosher salt
- 2 teaspoons ground black pepper
- 1 teaspoon paprika
- 2 teaspoons garlic powder
- 1 tablespoon honey
- 1 tablespoon cayenne pepper

DIRECTIONS

1 For the chicken: Preheat the air fryer to 375°F.

2 In a bowl, combine the mayonnaise, salt, paprika, sugar, turmeric, garlic powder, dried onion, thyme, mustard, cayenne, lemon peel, black pepper, and olive oil. Mix well. Brush the chicken evenly on all sides with mixture. Place the chicken on the air fryer shelf or in the air fryer basket. Cook for 35 minutes or until internal temperature of the meat has reached 165°F.

3 For the hot sauce: While the chicken is cooking, melt the butter in a sauce pan over medium-high heat. Add the brown sugar, salt, black pepper, paprika, garlic powder, honey, and cayenne. Stir until well combined, then remove from heat.

4 Remove chicken from air fryer and cut into pieces. Place on a serving platter and pour the hot sauce over the chicken.

> **ERIC SAYS:** Spatchcocking the chicken allows the whole bird to cook at the same time without the breast drying out. Use a good pair of kitchen shears to remove the backbone if one is not available ready-made at the market.

CRISPY BRAUHAUS TENDERS

SERVES 2 TO 4

INGREDIENTS

1 cup all-purpose flour

1 teaspoon garlic powder

1 teaspoon onion powder

1 tablespoon paprika

1 teaspoon salt

½ teaspoon pepper

2 eggs

¼ cup dark beer

2 cups crushed pretzels

1 pound chicken tenders

Cooking spray

Dipping sauce, for serving

DIRECTIONS

1 In a shallow dish, combine the flour, garlic powder, onion powder, paprika, salt, and pepper. Beat eggs with beer in a second shallow dish. Place pretzels in a third shallow dish.

2 Dredge chicken in flour mixture, dip in egg mixture, then again in flour mixture. Dip again in egg mixture, then roll in the crushed pretzels. Repeat process until all chicken is coated, placing chicken on a plate or tray as you work.

3 Spray air fryer shelves or basket with cooking spray and arrange chicken in fryer, being sure not to overcrowd. (Cook chicken in batches if necessary.) Cook at 400°F for 15 to 18 minutes, turning halfway through the cooking time, until golden brown.

4 Serve with your favorite dipping sauce.

ERIC SAYS: Don't forget the creamy beer cheese sauce for dunking these chicken tenders!

NASHVILLE TSO SANDWICH

MAKES 4

INGREDIENTS

- 4 chicken boneless, skinless chicken breasts
- 2 cups buttermilk
- 1 cup all-purpose flour
- 2 teaspoons salt
- 1 teaspoon pepper
- 2 cups crushed cornflakes
- Cooking spray
- 8 slices white sandwich bread
- Sliced dill pickles

FOR THE SAUCE

- ½ cup vegetable oil
- 2 tablespoons cayenne pepper
- 1 tablespoon smoked paprika
- 1 tablespoon dark chili powder
- 2 tablespoons brown sugar
- 3 tablespoons soy sauce
- 2 tablespoons rice vinegar
- 2 cloves chopped garlic
- 1 tablespoon grated fresh ginger
- ¼ cup orange juice concentrate

DIRECTIONS

1 **For the chicken:** Marinate the chicken in buttermilk in the refrigerator for 30 minutes to overnight.

2 **For the sauce:** Combine all sauce ingredients in a small saucepan and bring to a simmer over medium heat. Reduce heat to low and keep warm.

3 Remove chicken and place on a plate or platter, reserving the buttermilk. Mix flour, salt, and pepper in a bowl. Place crushed cornflakes in a second bowl. Dredge chicken in flour, dip in the buttermilk, then again in flour, then again in buttermilk. Roll in cornflakes to coat.

4 Spray air fryer shelves or basket with cooking spray and arrange chicken in fryer. Cook at 375°F for 20 minutes, turning halfway through the cooking time, or until meat reaches an internal temperature of 165°F.

5 Remove chicken from air fryer and brush with a heavy coat of sauce while it's still hot.

6 Serve on bread with pickles.

ERIC SAYS: If the heat isn't your thing, substitute sweet paprika for the cayenne. I I also dip this in a little blue cheese dressing to cool things down a bit.

PROSCIUTTO-GORGONZOLA ROLLATINI

MAKES 4

INGREDIENTS

- 4 boneless, skinless breasts, pounded to and ⅛-inch thickness
- 4 slices prosciutto
- ½ cup crumbled Gorgonzola cheese
- 2 tablespoons chopped fresh basil
- 1 tablespoons chopped garlic
- 3 tablespoons chopped sun-dried tomatoes
- 2 eggs,
- ¼ cup milk
- ½ cup all-purpose flour
- 2 cups seasoned breadcrumbs
- Cooking spray
- 1 (15-ounce) jar prepared Alfredo or marinara sauce, warmed

DIRECTIONS

1 Lay chicken breasts on a work surface. Top with prosciutto, then evenly divide the Gorgonzola, basil, garlic, and sun-dried tomatoes among them. Tightly roll up chicken and secure with a toothpick.

2 In a medium bowl, whisk together eggs and milk. Place flour in a second bowl and breadcrumbs in a third bowl. Dip each rolled breast in the egg mixture, then in the flour to coat. Dip again in egg mixture, then roll in breadcrumbs to coat.

3 Spray air fryer shelves or basket with cooking spray and arrange chicken in fryer. Cook at 350°F for 25 minutes or until meat reaches an internal temperature of 165°F.

4 Serve with warm Alfredo or marinara sauce.

> **ERIC SAYS:** I love to serve these rolls on top of a nice bed of spaghetti with either Alfredo or tomato sauce.

SANTORINI CHICKEN PITA

SERVES 4

INGREDIENTS

- 1 pound chicken breast, boneless and skinless, cut into strips
- 3 tablespoons olive oil
- 2 tablespoons fresh lemon juice
- 1 teaspoon fresh oregano
- ½ teaspoon fresh thyme, chopped
- 1 tablespoon fresh garlic, chopped
- ½ teaspoon salt
- ½ teaspoon pepper
- 4 pita bread
- 2 cups shredded lettuce
- 2 tablespoons red wine vinegar
- ½ cup onion, sliced
- ½ cup tomato, chopped
- ½ cup cucumber, sliced thin
- ½ cup crumbled feta
- Cooking spray

DIRECTIONS

1 In a small bowl, combine onion, tomato, cucumber and red wine vinegar. Set aside.

2 Combine olive oil, lemon juice, oregano, thyme, garlic, salt and pepper in a bowl. Add chicken strips and marinade for 15 minutes.

3 Spray air fryer shelves or basket with nonstick cooking spray and arrange chicken. Place the chicken into the air fryer and cook at 375ºF for about 8 to 10 minutes.

4 Warm the pitas and sprinkle lettuce over the them. Place hot chicken strips on top of lettuce. Top with the set aside vegetable mixture and feta cheese. Roll into a cone shape and serve.

> **ERIC SAYS:** Try substituting the pitas for bibb or romaine lettuce leaves and make a wrap if you are looking to lighten up the recipe.

SPICY TORTA MILANESE

SERVES 4

INGREDIENTS

- 2 cups panko breadcrumbs
- ¼ cup grated Parmesan cheese
- 2 cups finely shredded cabbage
- 2 tablespoons fresh lime juice
- 2 tablespoons chopped fresh cilantro
- 2 eggs
- ¼ cup all-purpose flour
- 4 chicken cutlets
- Cooking spray
- 2 teaspoons minced chipotle chiles in adobo sauce
- ¼ cup mayonnaise
- 4 Kaiser rolls, sliced
- 1 ripe avocado, mashed
- 1 cup crumbled queso fresco

DIRECTIONS

1 In a shallow bowl, combine panko and Parmesan cheese; set aside. In another bowl, combine the cabbage, lime juice, and cilantro; set aside. In a third bowl, beat the eggs. Place flour in a shallow dish.

2 Dust chicken cutlets with flour. Dip in beaten eggs, then dredge in the panko mixture, pressing to adhere.

3 Spray air fryer shelves or basket with cooking spray. Place the cutlets in the air fryer and cook at 350°F for 15 to 18 minutes or until golden brown, turning halfway through the cooking time. (If using a basket-style fryer, cook in batches.)

4 When ready to serve, stir together the chipotle chiles and mayonnaise. Spread on the bottom of each roll. Spread avocado on top of each roll. Divide cabbage mixture among roll bottoms. Top with chicken cutlets and cheese.

ROLLED PARMESAN-CRUSTED CHICKEN SALTIMBOCCA

SERVES 4

INGREDIENTS

FOR THE CHICKEN

- 4 boneless chicken cutlets
- ½ cup butter, softened
- 2 teaspoons dried basil
- 1 teaspoon pepper
- 8 slices prosciutto
- 4 whole-milk mozzarella string cheese
- 2 large eggs
- ¼ cup milk
- 1 cup almond flour
- 2 cups Parmesan cheese
- 1½ teaspoons garlic powder
- Cooking spray
- Fresh basil leaves, torn
- Lemon wedges

FOR THE LEMON BUTTER SAUCE

- 4 tablespoons butter
- 2 tablespoons lemon juice
- 1 clove garlic, minced
- ¼ cup chicken broth
- Cracked pepper to taste

DIRECTIONS

1 **For the chicken:** Spread butter on one side of the chicken, then sprinkle with dried basil and pepper.

2 Lay two slices of prosciutto and a piece of string cheese on each cutlet. Tightly roll up chicken and secure with toothpicks.

3 In a small bowl, beat eggs and milk. Place almond flour in a shallow dish. Stir together the Parmesan and garlic powder in second shallow dish. Dip each cutlet in almond the flour, then in the egg mixture, then in Parmesan mix. Dip again in the egg mixture, then dip in Parmesan again.

4 Spray air fryer rack or basket with cooking spray and arrange chicken in fryer. Cook at 375°F for 25 minutes or until center of roll reaches an internal temperature of 165°F.

5 **For the butter sauce:** Combine all sauce ingredients in a small saucepan. Cook and stir over low heat until butter has melted, 2 to 4 minutes.

6 Spoon sauce over chicken and sprinkle with fresh basil. Serve with lemon wedges.

ERIC SAYS: This dish pairs extremely well with warmed cannellini beans tossed in extra-virgin olive oil, fresh basil, and a little red chili flake.

MOROCCAN CHICKEN THIGHS

SERVES 2 TO 4

INGREDIENTS

FOR THE CHICKEN

Cooking spray

¾ cup mayonnaise

½ teaspoon brown sugar

½ teaspoon ground coriander

½ teaspoon ground cumin

½ teaspoon paprika

¼ teaspoon cinnamon

⅛ teaspoon salt

⅛ teaspoon pepper

4 bone-in chicken thighs

FOR THE SAUCE

3 shallots, chopped

¾ cup chicken broth, plus more if needed

4 pitted dates, chopped

1 teaspoon potato flakes

2 teaspoons fresh cilantro, minced

FOR THE COUSCOUS

3 tablespoons chicken broth

⅛ teaspoon salt

Dash ground cumin

⅓ cup uncooked couscous

2 teaspoons slivered almonds, toasted

DIRECTIONS

1 **For the chicken:** Spray air fryer racks or basket with cooking spray. Preheat air fryer at 375°F for 2 minutes.

2 In a bowl, combine mayonnaise, brown sugar, coriander, cumin, paprika, cinnamon, salt, and pepper. Mix well. Brush over chicken thighs.

3 Using tongs, place the chicken in the air fryer. Cook for 35 minutes or until the internal temperature of the meat reaches 165°F. While chicken is cooking, prepare the sauce and couscous .

4 **For the sauce:** Combine shallots, the ¾ cup broth, dates, potato flakes, and cilantro in a small saucepan. Bring to boiling over medium-high heat, stirring constantly, Reduce heat to a simmer and cook for about 6 minutes, being careful to not let it get too thick. Add small amounts of broth as needed. Keep warm until ready to serve.

5 **For the couscous:** In a small saucepan, bring ¼ cup water, broth, salt, and cumin to a boil. Stir in couscous. Cover and remove from heat. Let stand for about 10 min or until liquid has been absorbed. Fluff with a fork and stir in the almonds.

6 To serve, divide the couscous among plates or place on a serving platter. Place chicken on top of couscous and pour sauce over all.

> **ERIC SAYS:** Leftovers next day are amazing. I shred the chicken and mix it into the couscous, then roll it up burrito style with some baby arugula for a delicious wrap!

CALLIN' ALL
MEAT LOVERS

BLUE CHEESE-CRUSTED BEEF TENDERLOIN STEAKS

SERVES 2

INGREDIENTS

- 1 tablespoon butter, room temperature
- ½ cup panko breadcrumbs
- 1½ teaspoons dried parsley flakes
- ¼ teaspoon salt, plus more for seasoning
- 2 ounces crumbled blue cheese
- 2 (1½-inch-thick) beef tenderloin steaks
- Vegetable oil
- Pepper

DIRECTIONS

1 Preheat air fryer to 400°F for 4 minutes. Combine the butter, breadcrumbs, parsley flakes, and the ¼ teaspoon salt in a bowl. Gently fold in the blue cheese. Brush the steaks with oil and season to taste with salt and pepper

2 Cook steaks for 5 minutes, then turn and cook for an additional 5 minutes. Top with blue cheese mixture, then cook for an additional 5 minutes or until crust is golden brown.

3 Let steaks rest for 10 minutes before serving.

NOTE: This timing is for medium-rare doneness. Add additional minutes for a more well-done steak.

> **ERIC SAYS:** My side of choice for this dish is a creamy fettuccine Alfredo with fresh basil.

ARROSTICINI LAMB SKEWERS WITH LEMON-GARLIC AIOLI

SERVES 4

INGREDIENTS

1 cup olive oil

1 tablespoon fresh rosemary leaves

2 teaspoons salt

1 teaspoon black pepper

1 teaspoons red pepper flakes

1½ pounds lamb shoulder, cut into 2- to 3-inch cubes

½ cup mayonnaise

2 tablespoons lemon juice

1 tablespoon minced garlic

Skewers (if using wood skewers, soak in water 30 minutes before assembling)

DIRECTIONS

1 In a large bowl or platter, whisk together olive oil, rosemary, salt, black pepper, and red pepper flakes.

2 Carefully slide 8 pieces of lamb onto each skewer, securing them close to one another but not touching. Lay skewers in olive oil mixture, turning to coat, and let stand for at least 20 minutes, turning occasionally.

3 Place skewers on air fryer rack or in the basket. Cook at 400°F for 12 minutes, turning halfway through the cooking time. (Cook in batches if necessary.)

4 While lamb is cooking, combine mayonnaise, lemon juice, and garlic in a small bowl.

5 Serve lamb skewers with aioli over rice, grilled vegetables, or a green salad.

> **ERIC SAYS:** I love serving these kebabs over turmeric rice with dried dates and dried apricots to give a sweet floral flavor profile.

PISTACHIO & MINT-CRUSTED LAMB LOIN

SERVES 4 TO 6

INGREDIENTS

- ¼ cup olive oil
- 2 cups unsalted pistachio nuts, shelled and roughly chopped
- ¼ cup chopped fresh mint
- 2 teaspoons salt
- 1 teaspoon pepper
- 1½ teaspoons chopped fresh rosemary
- 1 boneless lamb loin (about 2 pounds)

DIRECTIONS

1 In a small bowl, combine olive oil, pistachio nuts, mint, salt and pepper. Rub mixture all over lamb loin, coating all of the meat.

2 Place on air fryer rack or in air fryer basket. Cook at 375°F for 40 minutes, flipping halfway through until internal temperature of loin reaches 145°F.

3 Let rest 5 to 10 minutes before slicing.

> **ERIC SAYS:** This is so French bistro. Serve lamb over a chilled greens salad with poached pears, crumbled goat cheese and sliced dried figs. Drizzle with olive oil and rice wine vinegar.

CURRIED LAMB BURGERS WITH APRICOT YOGURT SAUCE & CARAMELIZED ONIONS

SERVES 4

INGREDIENTS

- 4 tablespoons olive oil, divided
- 1 cup chopped onion
- 1 tablespoon grated fresh ginger
- 2 teaspoons salt, divided
- 2 teaspoons curry powder
- 1½ pounds ground lamb
- 5 tablespoons chopped fresh cilantro, divided
- 1½ teaspoons cracked black pepper, divided
- ¾ cup plain whole-milk Greek yogurt
- ½ cup apricot jam
- 3 tablespoons chopped fresh mint
- Zest from ½ lime
- Coarse salt
- 1 large yellow onion, sliced
- Cooking spray
- Baby arugula
- 4 hamburger buns

DIRECTIONS

1 Heat 2 tablespoons oil in large skillet over medium heat. Add chopped onion, ginger, and ½ teaspoon salt. Sauté until onion is tender, about 8 minutes. Add curry powder and stir 30 seconds. Remove from heat. Cool onion mixture to room temperature, at least 15 minutes.

2 Place lamb in large bowl. Add onion mixture, 1 teaspoon salt, 3 tablespoons of the cilantro, and 1 teaspoon cracked pepper. Blend mixture gently; shape into four ½-inch-thick patties.

3 Mix yogurt, apricot jam, mint, remaining 2 tablespoons cilantro, and lime zest in a small bowl. Season to taste with coarse salt and remaining ½ teaspoon cracked pepper. Cover; chill until cold, at least 30 minutes.

4 In a large saucepan, heat remaining 2 tablespoons olive oil. Add sliced onions and remaining ½ teaspoon salt to pan. Cook over low heat, stirring continuously, until onions have developed a deep brown color.

5 Spray air fryer rack or basket with cooking spray. Place burgers in air fryer. Cook at 375°F for 30 minutes, flipping halfway through cooking time, or until meat reaches an internal temperature of 160°F.

6 **To assemble:** Place patties on bun bottoms. Top with yogurt sauce, caramelized onions, and arugula. Top with bun tops.

> **ERIC SAYS:** You can divide the burgers into smaller pieces and form them into ovals. Serve with crisp bibb lettuce to make wraps!

PASTRAMI SPICED SIRLOIN STEAK WITH RUSSIAN DRESSING COLESLAW

SERVES 4

INGREDIENTS

FOR THE SLAW

¾ cup mayonnaise

⅓ cup cocktail sauce

⅓ cup minced onion

2 teaspoon Worcestershire sauce

¾ teaspoon smoked paprika

1 tablespoon white vinegar

1 (14 ounce) bag coleslaw mix

FOR THE STEAKS

1 tablespoon kosher salt

1 tablespoon brown sugar

1 tablespoon coarse-ground pepper

2 teaspoons paprika

2 teaspoons whole mustard seeds, crushed

1 teaspoon granulated garlic

1 teaspoon granulated onion

1 teaspoon ground coriander

4 (6-ounce) sirloin steaks

Cooking spray

DIRECTIONS

1 **For the slaw:** Combine the mayonnaise, cocktail sauce, onion, Worcestershire sauce, paprika, and vinegar in a large bowl. Add the coleslaw mix to bowl and toss to coat. Cover and refrigerate until serving time.

2 **For the steaks:** Combine the kosher salt, brown sugar, pepper, paprika, mustard seeds, granulated garlic, granulated onion and coriander in a bowl. Rub steaks generously with spice mix on both sides. Place on a plate and marinate in the refrigerator, uncovered, for 2 hours.

3 Spray air fryer rack or basket with cooking spray. Place the steaks in air fryer. Cook at 370°F for 10 minutes, turn, and cook for 5 minutes more. Let steak rest for 5 minutes (Cook steaks in batches if necessary.)

4 Serve steaks with coleslaw.

> **ERIC SAYS:** These make great party hors d'oeuvres—slice the steak super-thin and make mini street tacos topped with the coleslaw.

JAMAICAN JERK-RUBBED LAMB CHOPS WITH FRESH MANGO CHUTNEY

SERVES 3 TO 4

INGREDIENTS

FOR THE LAMB

- 2 tablespoons olive oil
- 1 tablespoon dried onion flakes
- 1 teaspoon ground thyme
- 1 teaspoon dried parsley
- 1 teaspoon ground allspice
- 1 teaspoon nutmeg
- 1 teaspoon onion powder
- 1½ teaspoons cumin
- 1 teaspoon turmeric
- 1 teaspoon garlic powder
- 2 teaspoons salt
- 1 teaspoon black pepper
- ½ teaspoon cayenne pepper
- 2 teaspoons paprika
- ½ teaspoon red pepper flakes
- ⅓ cup brown sugar
- 8 lamb rib chops
- Cooking spray

FOR THE CHUTNEY

- 2 cups diced fresh mango
- ¾ cup diced red bell pepper
- ¼ cup diced red onion, diced
- ¼ cup chopped cilantro
- ½ cup lime juice
- Salt and pepper

DIRECTIONS

1 For the lamb: In a medium bowl, combine the olive oil, onion flakes, thyme, parsley, allspice, nutmeg, onion powder, cumin, turmeric, garlic powder, salt, black pepper, cayenne, paprika, red pepper flakes, and brown sugar. Mix well to combine. Rub generously all over lamb chops. Cover and refrigerate for at least 2 hours.

2 For the chutney: In a medium bowl, combine mango, red pepper, red onion, cilantro, and lime juice. Season with salt and pepper to taste. Chill until serving time.

3 Spray air fryer racks or basket with cooking spray. Arrange lamb chops in fryer. (Cook in batches if necessary.) Cook at 375°F for 6 to 8 minutes or until meat reaches an internal temperature reaches 135°F (medium), turning halfway through cooking time to ensure browning.

4 Serve chops with fresh mango chutney.

ERIC SAYS: Rice and peas is a Jamaican food staple. It pairs beautifully with this lamb recipe. I love to add a little coconut milk to the rice and really accentuate that island flavor.

BEEF ROLL UPS

SERVES 2 TO 3

INGREDIENTS

- 3 cloves garlic, minced
- 1 tablespoon fresh chopped rosemary or 1½ teaspoons dried rosemary, crushed
- 1 teaspoon salt
- ¼ teaspoon pepper
- ¼ cup olive oil
- 1 pound top round beef cutlets
- ½ cup Italian-seasoned breadcrumbs
- ¼ cup grated Parmesan cheese
- Cooking spray

DIRECTIONS

1 Stir together the garlic, rosemary, salt, pepper, and olive oil in a small bowl. Slice cutlets into 4- to 5-inch long pieces. Rub the olive oil mixture on the sliced cutlets. Cover and marinate in the refrigerator for 2 to 3 hours.

2 Mix together the breadcrumbs and the cheese in a shallow dish. Press both sides of beef pieces into the breadcrumb mixture, coating well. Roll up and secure with a toothpick.

3 Spray air fryer racks or basket with cooking spray. Arrange rolls in fryer and cook at 375°F for 18 minutes, turning once or twice. (Cooking in batches if necessary.)

4 Remove toothpicks before serving.

> **ERIC SAYS:** I always crave a hearty mushroom risotto when I see recipes like this—and don't forget the sautéed spinach!

BACON-WRAPPED PORTOBELLO MUSHROOMS WITH GOAT CHEESE BRUSCHETTA

SERVES 2

INGREDIENTS

- ¼ cup + 1 tablespoon balsamic vinegar
- 1 cup + 2 tablespoons olive oil
- 1 teaspoon pepper, plus more to taste
- 1 teaspoon dried oregano
- ½ teaspoon dried basil
- 2 large portobello mushroom caps, gills scraped out
- 10 bacon thin-cut bacon strips
- ¼ cup butter, melted
- Cooking spray
- 1 cup grape tomatoes, halved
- ½ cup crumbled goat cheese
- ¼ cup fresh basil leaves, thinly sliced
- Salt

DIRECTIONS

1 In a large airtight container, combine the ¼ cup balsamic vinegar, 1 cup olive oil, 1 teaspoon pepper, oregano, and basil. Place the mushroom caps in the marinade and stir to coat well. Cover and marinate in the refrigerator for at least 2 hours. When ready to cook, remove mushrooms from marinade and pat dry with a paper towel.

2 On a work surface, lay 5 strips of bacon in an asterisk design. Place a mushroom cap top side down in the center of bacon and fold each piece up into the center. Tuck bacon into the center and brush bacon pieces with melted butter. Repeat with other mushroom.

3 Spray air fryer rack or basket with cooking spray. Place mushrooms in fryer and cook at 370°F for 10 minutes, rotating halfway through cooking time, until bacon is crispy and golden. Using tongs, remove mushrooms and allow to cool slightly.

4 In a medium bowl, combine tomatoes, goat cheese, basil, 1 tablespoon balsamic vinegar, and remaining 2 tablespoons olive oil. Season with salt and pepper to taste.

5 Divide goat cheese mixture between mushroom caps and serve.

> **ERIC SAYS:** Serve burger-style on a buttery brioche bun and crisp shredded iceberg lettuce!

CARIBBEAN-SPICED STUFFED PEPPERS

MAKES 6

INGREDIENTS

3 large bell peppers, halved, stemmed, and seeded

Cooking spray

1 pound ground beef

¾ cup chopped onion

2 tablespoons Jamaican jerk seasoning

1½ cups cooked rice

2 ounces cream cheese

1¾ cups shredded mozzarella

1 (8-ounce) can crushed pineapple, drained

½ cup ketchup

1 tablespoon red wine vinegar

1 tablespoon brown sugar

DIRECTIONS

1 Spray pepper halves with cooking spray and place flesh side down in air fryer. Cook at 400°F for 5 minutes. Remove peppers from fryer and let cool.

2 Cook ground beef and onion in a skillet over medium-high heat. Drain and transfer to a bowl. Stir in jerk seasoning, rice, cream cheese, and 1 cup of mozzarella. Fill pepper halves with beef mixture.

3 Arrange pepper halves in air fryer and cook at 350°F for 15 minutes. (Cook in batches if necessary.) During the last 3 minutes of cooking time, top peppers with remaining cheese and cook until cheese is browned.

4 While peppers are cooking, combine pineapple, ketchup, vinegar, and brown sugar in a saucepan. Heat over medium-low heat until sugar is dissolved. Serve peppers with sauce.

> **ERIC SAYS:** Try putting a pepper on a nice soft brioche burger bun, or cut it in half and stuff a crusty French baguette for an amazing sandwich!

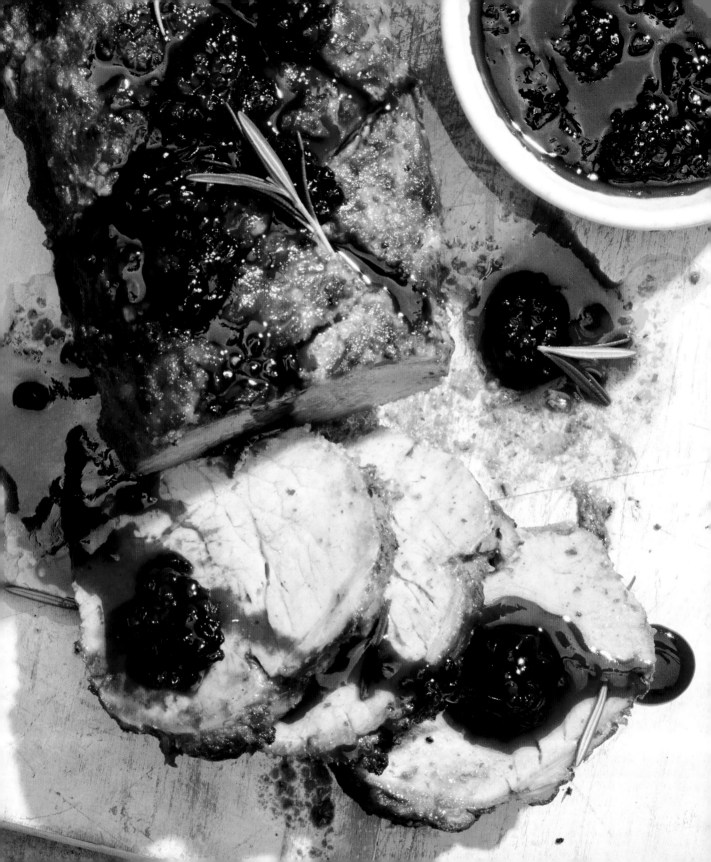

CREOLE PORK ROAST WITH BLACKBERRY SAUCE

SERVES 2 TO 4

INGREDIENTS

FOR THE MEAT

- 1 pork loin roast (about 3 pounds)
- ¼ cup Creole mustard
- 2 teaspoons paprika
- 2 teaspoons garlic powder
- 2 teaspoons onion powder
- 2 teaspoons dried parsley
- ½ teaspoon cayenne pepper
- 2 teaspoons salt
- 1 teaspoon black pepper
- Cooking spray

FOR THE SAUCE

- 3 cups fresh or frozen blackberries
- ½ cup sugar
- ⅓ cup orange juice
- 1 tablespoon apple cider vinegar

DIRECTIONS

1 Preheat air fryer at 375°F for 5 minutes. If using an oven-style fryer, place rack on the lowest shelf. Use the blade of a sharp chef's knife or the tip of a paring knife to score the surface of the pork in diamond shapes ¼ inch deep.

2 In a small bowl, combine mustard, paprika, garlic and onion powder, parsley, cayenne pepper, salt, and black pepper. Rub spice mixture all over the pork.

3 Spray a large piece of aluminum foil with cooking spray and wrap pork roast in foil.

4 Place roast in fryer and cook at 375°F for 45 minutes. Using an oven mitt, unwrap pork to allow roast to brown, and cook for an additional 15 minutes, or until the meat has reached an internal temperature of 145°F.

5 While pork is cooking, combine sauce ingredients in a small saucepan and bring to a boil. Reduce heat and simmer for 8 to 10 minutes or until sauce has thickened slightly.

6 Let roast rest 10 minutes before slicing. Serve sauce with pork.

ERIC SAYS: In keeping with the Southern theme, enjoy this with some grits and collard greens, You will not be disappointed!

SLOPPY JOE MEATLOAF

SERVES 4 TO 6

INGREDIENTS

FOR THE MEAT

- 1 cup soft breadcrumbs
- ¼ cup milk
- 1 pound ground beef
- ½ cup diced yellow onion
- ½ cup diced green pepper
- 1 large egg, beaten
- 2 tablespoons ketchup
- 1 tablespoon Worcestershire sauce
- 1 tablespoon yellow mustard
- 1 teaspoon chili powder
- ⅛ teaspoon cayenne pepper
- 1 teaspoon salt
- ¼ teaspoon garlic powder
- ¼ teaspoon black pepper

FOR THE GLAZE

- ½ cup ketchup
- ¼ cup packed light brown sugar
- 2 tablespoons red wine vinegar
- 2 teaspoons yellow mustard

DIRECTIONS

1 For the meat: Combine the breadcrumbs and milk in a large bowl and let sit for a minute or two. Add the ground beef, onion, green pepper, egg, ketchup, Worcestershire sauce, mustard, chili powder, cayenne, salt, garlic powder, and black pepper to bowl. Mix together until well combined.

2 Cut a piece of parchment paper to fit the air fryer rack or the bottom of the air fryer basket. Form the meat mixture into a loaf and place on the parchment paper. Place parchment with meatloaf on it into the air fryer. Cook at 375°F for 30 minutes.

3 For the glaze: While meatloaf is cooking, combine the ingredients for the glaze. After 30 minutes of cooking time, brush or spoon about half of the glaze on the meatloaf. Cook for 5 minutes more.

4 Serve meatloaf with reserved glaze.

> **ERIC SAYS:** Slice the meatloaf thin and grill with sharp cheddar cheese and between two pieces of Texas toast for an amazing grilled cheese!

ASIAN-STYLE PORK MEATLOAF

SERVES 4 TO 6

INGREDIENTS

- 2 pounds ground pork
- 3 garlic cloves, minced
- 1 tablespoon grated fresh ginger
- ¼ cup soy sauce
- 2 tablespoons chili-garlic sauce
- ½ cup diced red bell pepper
- ½ cup chopped scallions, plus more for garnish
- 2 teaspoons thinly sliced fresh mint
- 2 eggs, beaten
- 1 cup panko breadcrumbs
- Cooking spray
- ½ cup Asian-style barbecue sauce, plus more for serving

DIRECTIONS

1 In a large mixing bowl, combine pork, garlic, ginger, soy sauce, chili-garlic sauce, red pepper, ½ cup of the scallions, mint, eggs, and breadcrumbs. Mix well. Form meat mixture into a loaf.

2 Spray a sheet of aluminum foil with cooking spray. Place meat onto the foil. Place foil and meat onto air fryer rack or into the basket. Spray a second sheet of aluminum foil with cooking spray and place on top of meat, loosely molding the foil around it.

3 Cook at 350°F for 40 minutes. Using tongs, remove the top piece of foil and brush or spoon the ½ cup barbecue sauce on the meatloaf. Continue cooking, uncovered, until the internal temperature of the loaf reaches 160°F.

4 Remove meatloaf from fryer and let stand 5 to 10 minutes before serving. Garnish the top with scallions and serve with additional barbecue sauce.

> **ERIC SAYS:** Most Asian markets will have bao buns. Give them a quick steam, a little hoisin sauce, scallions, and you have Asian sliders!

STEAK PARMESAN

SERVES 2

INGREDIENTS

- ¼ cup all-purpose flour
- 1½ cups plain panko breadcrumbs
- 1½ teaspoons Italian seasoning
- ⅓ cup Parmesan cheese
- 1¼ teaspoons salt
- ¾ teaspoon pepper
- 2 eggs, beaten
- 2 (5-ounce) steaks
- Cooking spray
- 1 cup shredded mozzarella
- 1 cup marinara, warmed

DIRECTIONS

1 Place flour in a shallow dish. Combine the breadcrumbs, Italian seasoning, Parmesan cheese, salt, and pepper in another shallow dish. Place eggs in a third.

2 Lightly dredge one of the steaks in the flour. Dip it in egg, then coat with the breadcrumb mixture. Dip in egg again and again in the breadcrumb mixture. Set aside and repeat with the second steak.

3 Spray air fry rack or basket lightly with cooking spray. Preheat air fryer for 2 minutes at 375°F. Place steaks in fryer and cook for 12 to 14 minutes, flipping steaks and lightly spraying with cooking spray halfway through the cooking time.

4 Two minutes before the end of cooking time, top steaks with cheese, then continue to cook for 2 minutes.

5 Serve steaks with marinara sauce.

> **ERIC SAYS:** I love to serve this with garlicky broccoli rabe spiced with red pepper flakes!

5-SPICE STEAK WITH HORSERADISH-ROASTED MUSHROOMS

SERVES 3 TO 4

INGREDIENTS

1½ teaspoons 5-spice powder

1½ teaspoons brown sugar

1 teaspoon salt

½ teaspoon garlic powder, divided

½ teaspoon ground ginger, divided

1 pound flank or skirt steak

1 tablespoon olive oil

1 tablespoon balsamic vinegar

1 tablespoon soy sauce

1½ teaspoons prepared horseradish

8 ounces large mushrooms, stemmed trimmed, halved

Olive oil cooking spray

DIRECTIONS

1 Combine the 5-spice powder, brown sugar, salt, ¼ teaspoon of the garlic powder, and ¼ teaspoon of the ground ginger in a bowl. Rub the spice mixture all over the meat. Cover and let stand at room temperature for 30 minutes.

2 Preheat air fryer to 400°F for 2 minutes. In a large bowl, combine the remaining garlic powder and ground ginger, olive oil, balsamic vinegar, soy sauce, and horseradish. Add mushrooms ands toss to coat.

3 Spray steak with cooking spray and place in air fryer. Cook at 400°F for 15 to 20 minutes, turning halfway through the cooking time, and until meat reaches an internal temperature of 135°F (medium). Remove the steak the from fryer, cover with foil, and let rest while the mushrooms cook.

4 Add the mushrooms to the air fryer and cook at 400°F for an 8 to 10 minutes.

5 Slice steak thinly against the grain and serve with mushrooms.

ERIC SAYS: Chill leftovers and top a wedge salad with sliced steak and creamy blue cheese dressing!

KOREAN-STYLE BBQ BURGER WITH KIMCHI MAYO

MAKES 4

INGREDIENTS

FOR THE BURGERS

1½ pounds ground beef

½ cup chopped scallions

1 tablespoon grated fresh ginger

2 cloves garlic, minced

2 tablespoons brown sugar

2 tablespoons rice wine vinegar

3 tablespoons soy sauce

1 tablespoon toasted sesame oil

1½ teaspoons sesame seeds

1 teaspoon sriracha sauce

½ teaspoon salt

4 hamburger buns

Arugula or baby spinach

FOR THE KIMCHI MAYO

1 cup mayonnaise

½ cup kimchi, chopped

1 teaspoon brown sugar

2 tablespoons chopped scallions

DIRECTIONS

1 For the burgers: Mix together the ground beef, scallions, ginger, garlic, brown sugar, vinegar, soy sauce, sesame oil, sesame seeds, sriracha, and salt. Form into four ½-inch-thick burgers.

2 Preheat air fryer to 380°F for 2 minutes. Place burgers in fryer and cook at 380°F for 10 minutes, turning after 5 minutes. Continue cooking another 5 to 8 minutes, depending on desired doneness.

3 For the kimchi mayo: Stir together the mayonnaise, kimchi, brown sugar, and scallions.

4 Serve burgers on buns topped with kimchi mayo and arugula.

STUFFED PORK CHOPS WITH SMOKED GOUDA, APPLES & PINE NUTS

SERVES 2

INGREDIENTS

- 2 boneless thick-cut pork chops
- 1 cup shredded smoked Gouda cheese
- ¾ cup finely diced Granny Smith apples
- 2 tablespoons mayonnaise
- 1 garlic clove, minced
- 2 tablespoons pine nuts
- 2 tablespoons breadcrumbs
- 2 tablespoons dry mustard
- ½ teaspoon salt
- ½ teaspoon black pepper
- ½ teaspoon cayenne pepper
- Toothpicks

DIRECTIONS

1 Using a paring knife, make a 1-inch slit into a side of each of the pork chops, cutting into but not all of the way through, to create a pocket.

2 In a medium bowl, mix the cheese, apples, mayonnaise, garlic, pine nuts, and breadcrumbs. Gently stuff the pork chops with the mixture, using your fingers to push the mixture completely inside the pocket. Close opening with a toothpick. Chill for at least 30 minutes before cooking.

3 When ready to cook, mix the dry mustard, salt, black pepper, and cayenne pepper in a small dish. Rub mixture all over the outside of both pork chops.

4 Cook at 375°F for 30 minutes, turning halfway through the cooking time, or until the internal temperature of the pork reaches 145°F.

5 Allow pork to rest for 10 minutes and remove toothpicks before serving.

> **ERIC SAYS:** Complete this autumn dish with roasted Brussels sprouts and a baked sweet potato with maple and cinnamon.

PORK KATSUDON WITH YELLOW CURRY SAUCE & WHITE RICE

SERVES 2

INGREDIENTS

- 2 boneless pork cutlets, ¼ inch thick
- 1 cup all-purpose flour
- ½ teaspoon salt
- ½ teaspoon pepper
- 2 eggs
- 2 cups panko breadcrumbs
- Cooking spray
- 1 tablespoon olive oil
- 1 small onion, diced
- ½ diced carrots
- 2 teaspoons curry powder
- ½ teaspoon turmeric
- 2 garlic cloves, minced
- 1 teaspoon minced fresh ginger
- 1 cup chicken broth
- ½ cup coconut milk
- 2 tablespoons soy sauce
- 2 cups cooked white rice
- Sliced scallions for garnish

DIRECTIONS

1 In a shallow bowl, combine flour, salt, and pepper. In another bowl, beat eggs. Place the panko breadcrumbs in a third shallow bowl.

2 Dredge the cutlets in the flour mixture, dip in eggs, and then in breadcrumbs. Dip coated cutlets back into the eggs and again into the breadcrumbs two more times to ensure a thick crust.

3 Spray air fryer rack or basket with cooking spray. Cook coated cutlets at 360°F for 10 minutes or until pork reaches an internal temperature of 145°F and crust is golden brown, turning halfway through the cooking time.

4 While pork is cooking, heat the olive oil in a large saucepan over medium heat. Add onions and carrots and cook until softened. Add curry powder and turmeric. Stir to combine and cook for 2 minutes. Add garlic and ginger. Stir and cook for another minute. Add broth, coconut milk, and soy sauce and cook, stirring frequently, until sauce has thickened slightly.

5 Top rice with cutlets and curry sauce. Garnish with scallions.

> **ERIC SAYS:** Take this recipe to the next level by topping with a sunny-side up egg and a little kimchi!

ASIAN STEAK TIPS WITH SESAME-ROASTED SWEET POTATOES

SERVES 4

INGREDIENTS

- 3 tablespoons vegetable oil, divided
- 2 cloves garlic, minced
- 1 tablespoon grated fresh ginger
- 3 scallions, cut into 2-inch pieces
- ½ cup soy sauce
- ½ cup brown sugar
- 1 tablespoon rice wine vinegar
- ¼ cup water
- 1 tablespoon cornstarch
- 1½ pounds sirloin steak tips
- 1 pound sweet potatoes, peeled and cut into wedges
- 1 tablespoon toasted sesame oil
- 2 tablespoon sesame seeds, toasted

DIRECTIONS

1 Heat 1 tablespoon oil in a small saucepan over medium heat. Add the garlic, ginger, and scallions and sauté until fragrant. Add the soy sauce, brown sugar, and rice wine vinegar and bring to a simmer.

2 In a small bowl, stir together the water and cornstarch. Stir into the saucepan. Simmer until sauce thickens slightly. Keep warm until ready to serve.

3 Preheat air fryer at 400°F for 2 minutes. Toss the sirloin tips in 1 tablespoon oil and cook for 6 minutes, shaking basket or stirring halfway through the cooking time. Remove steak tips to a plate and cover loosely with foil.

4 Toss sweet potatoes in sesame oil and cook at 380°F for 12 minutes, stirring or tossing halfway through the cooking time.

5 Sprinkle sweet potatoes with sesame seeds and serve with steak tips and sauce.

> **ERIC SAYS:** You can make many variations of this dish just by swapping out different proteins. Try pork tenderloin, beef tenderloin, jumbo shrimp, or even scallops. Don't forget the sticky rice!

CHIPOTLE-SPICED PORK TENDERLOIN WITH SOUTHWEST SLAW

SERVES 4

INGREDIENTS

FOR THE PORK

- 1 tablespoon chipotle powder
- 1 tablespoon paprika
- ½ teaspoon pepper
- 2 cloves garlic, minced
- 1 teaspoon salt
- 1 pork tenderloin (1½ to 2 lbs)

FOR THE SLAW

- 1½ cups cooked black beans
- 1 cup fresh or frozen corn kernels
- 1 cup very thinly sliced red pepper
- ½ cup finely diced red onion
- 2 tablespoons chopped fresh cilantro
- Salt and pepper
- ⅔ cup mayonnaise
- 1 tablespoon hot sauce
- Lime wedges for garnish

DIRECTIONS

1 For the pork: Combine chipotle powder, paprika, pepper, minced garlic, and salt in a small bowl. Coat pork loin with mixture. Wrap in plastic and refrigerate for at least 1 hour.

2 Before cooking, allow pork to sit at room temperature for 15 minutes. Cook at 375°F for 30 minutes or until pork reaches an internal temperature of 145°F. Let rest for 10 minutes before slicing.

3 For the slaw: In a large bowl combine beans, corn, red pepper, onion, cilantro, and salt and pepper to taste. In a small bowl, whisk together mayonnaise and hot sauce. Drizzle over slaw mixture and mix to combine. Refrigerate until ready to serve.

4 Serve pork with slaw and lime wedges.

ERIC SAYS: You can also let it cool overnight in the fridge then slice it super thin and make a delicious sandwich. I will take a crusty baguette, baby arugula and slaw, delicious!

OPEN-FACED CUBAN SANDWICHES WITH PICADILLO RELISH

SERVES 4

INGREDIENTS

½ cup onion, chopped

½ cup dill pickle, chopped

½ cup Spanish olives, chopped

¼ raisins, chopped

2 tablespoons yellow mustard

2 tablespoons mayonnaise

4 slices sourdough bread

4 slices deli ham

8 slices deli roast pork loin

4 slices Swiss cheese

DIRECTIONS

1 In a small bowl, combine the onion, pickle, olives, raisins, mustard, and mayonnaise. Thickly spread relish over bread slices, reserving some for serving if desired.

2 Top each with 1 slice ham, 2 slices pork loin, and 1 slice cheese. Place the sandwiches in the air fryer and cook at 370°F for 10 minutes or until the cheese is bubbling and starting to brown. (Cook in batches if necessary.)

3 Serve with any remaining relish.

ERIC SAYS: I love to put a tropical twist on the picadillo relish by adding some fresh ripe mango. The sweet complements the brine of the olives.

SOUTHERN CORNMEAL-CRUSTED CALAMARI WITH ZESTY REMOULADE

SERVES 2 TO 4

INGREDIENTS

FOR THE CALAMARI

- ½ cup corn flour
- ½ cup corn meal
- 1 tablespoon garlic powder
- 1 tablespoon onion powder
- ½ teaspoon cayenne pepper
- 1 teaspoon salt, plus more to taste
- ½ teaspoon black pepper, plus more to taste
- 1 pound calamari, fresh or frozen, thawed, rinsed and drained
- Cooking spray

FOR THE REMOULADE

- ½ cup mayonnaise
- 2 tablespoons capers, chopped, plus 1 teaspoon brine
- 1 teaspoon fresh lemon juice
- 1 tablespoon minced red onion
- 1 tablespoon chopped fresh dill

DIRECTIONS

1 For the calamari: In a large bowl, combine the corn flour, corn meal, spices, the 1 teaspoon salt and ½ teaspoon pepper. Stir to combine. Toss calamari in breading mixture, ensuring all pieces are completely coated.

2 Spray air fryer rack or basket with cooking spray. Place calamari in a single layer in fryer. Cook at 375º F for 10 to 12 minutes, turning or shaking halfway through cooking time to ensure even browning.

3 For the remoulade: While calamari is cooking, in a medium bowl, combine the mayonnaise, capers and brine, lemon juice, red onions, dill, and salt and pepper to taste. Stir to combine. Cover and chill until ready to serve.

4 Serve calamari for calamari.

> **ERIC SAYS:** Get some crusty Italian bread, dress it with the remoulade, lettuce, and tomato. Pack in the crispy calamari and you just made a New Orleans Po' Boy!

CITRUS-SPICED SEA SCALLOPS WITH ROASTED ASPARAGUS

SERVES 2 TO 3

INGREDIENTS

¼ cup olive oil, divided

¼ cup fresh lemon juice, divided

¼ cup fresh lime juice, divided

1 tablespoon lemon zest, divided

1 tablespoon lime zest, divided

1 teaspoon pepper, divided

¼ cup tequila

2 teaspoons salt

1 pound sea scallops, fresh or frozen, thawed

1 pound asparagus, trimmed

DIRECTIONS

1 Divide the olive oil, lemon juice, lime juice, lemon zest, lime zest, and pepper between two gallon-size resealable plastic bags. Add the tequila to one bag. Place the scallops in the bag with the tequila and the asparagus in the other bag. Seal and massage to coat. Marinate in the refrigerator for 1 hour, turning once.

2 Drain marinade from both scallops and asparagus. Pat scallops dry with a paper towel, then season scallops and asparagus with the salt.

3 For an air fryer oven: Place scallops on air fryer rack towards the bottom of the oven. Place asparagus on air fryer rack towards the top of the oven. Cook at 375°F for 8 to 10 minutes, rotating racks halfway through the cooking time, until scallops have a deep brown crust. (Asparagus may be done before scallops—remove and keep warm until scallops are done cooking).For an air fryer basket: Arrange asparagus around outer rim of the basket and place scallops inside the center. Cook at 375°F for 8 to 10 minutes. Use tongs to turns asparagus and scallops halfway through the cooking time.

> **ERIC SAYS:** I love to serve the scallops and asparagus over pasta with a lemon-caper cream sauce.

SPICY SOY-GLAZED SALMON WITH ASIAN SLAW

SERVES 4

INGREDIENTS

½ cup soy sauce

¼ cup orange juice

1 teaspoon minced fresh ginger

1 clove garlic, minced

4 salmon fillets, skin on

1½ cups shredded napa cabbage

1 cup shredded purple cabbage

½ cup shredded carrots

½ cup chopped scallions

2 tablespoons chopped fresh cilantro

¾ cup mayonnaise

2 tablespoons sriracha sauce

3 tablespoons lime juice

1 teaspoon pepper

DIRECTIONS

1 In a small saucepan, combine soy sauce, orange juice, ginger, and garlic. Cook over medium heat until sauce is reduced by half and has the consistency of a thick glaze.

2 Pat salmon with a paper towel to remove excess moisture. Generously brush each piece of salmon with soy glaze. Place fish in air fryer. Cook at 350°F for 15 to 20 minutes, brushing with additional glaze once or twice, until salmon reaches an internal temperature of 145°F.

3 In a large bowl, combine cabbage, carrots, scallions and cilantro. In a small bowl, stir together the mayonnaise, sriracha, lime juice and pepper. Add mayonnaise sauce to vegetable mixture. Toss to combine.

4 Serve slaw with salmon.

> **ERIC SAYS:** Grab a large flour tortilla, warm sushi rice, and roll it up with the salmon and slaw. You will never look at burritos the same way again!

COCONUT-ALMOND TILAPIA WITH SWEET CHILI MANGO SALSA

SERVES 2

INGREDIENTS

- ¼ cup all-purpose flour
- 1 teaspoon salt
- ¼ teaspoon pepper
- 2 eggs
- ½ cup shredded coconut, lightly toasted
- ½ cup almonds, finely ground
- ½ cup panko breadcrumbs
- 2 (6-ounce) tilapia fillets
- Cooking spray
- ¾ cup finely diced mango
- ¼ cup finely diced red pepper
- ¼ cup finely diced red onion
- 2 tablespoons sweet chili sauce
- 2 tablespoons mayonnaise
- 2 tablespoons chopped fresh cilantro
- 2 teaspoons lime juice

DIRECTIONS

1 Stir together the flour, salt, and pepper in a shallow dish. Beat eggs in a second shallow dish. Stir together the coconut, almonds, and breadcrumbs in a third shallow dish.

2 Pat the tilapia dry with a paper towel. Dredge fillets in the flour, then egg. Coat with the coconut mixture.

3 Preheat air fryer at 390°F for 2 minutes. Place the fillets in air fryer and spray with cooking spray. Cook for 8 minutes, turning halfway through the cooking time.

4 While fish is cooking, combine the mango, red pepper, red onion, chili sauce, mayonnaise, cilantro, and lime juice in a bowl.

5 Serve fish with the salsa.

> **ERIC SAYS:** This recipe screams fish tacos! I prefer mine on corn tortillas, with a little shredded cabbage and guac!

SALMON BORDELAISE

SERVES 4

INGREDIENTS

- 4 tablespoons butter, room temperature
- 2 cloves garlic, minced
- 2 tablespoons lemon juice
- 2 tablespoons chopped fresh parsley
- ½ teaspoon dried thyme
- ½ teaspoon salt
- ¼ teaspoon smoked paprika
- ¼ teaspoon pepper
- 1 tablespoon Creole seasoning
- 4 (6-ounce) salmon fillets
- Cooking spray

DIRECTIONS

1 For the bordelaise butter, combine the butter, garlic, lemon juice, parsley, thyme, salt, smoked paprika, and pepper; set aside.

2 Season the salmon fillets with the Creole seasoning.

3 Spray air fryer rack or basket with cooking spray. Place salmon, skin side down, in the air fryer. Spray each fillet with a light coating of cooking spray. Cook at 390°F for 8 minutes or until fish flakes with a fork.

4 When ready to serve, top each fillet with a tablespoon of the bordelaise butter.

COCONUT-CRUSTED FISH FILLETS

SERVES 4

INGREDIENTS

Cooking spray

4 whitefish fillets, such as grouper or haddock

¼ cup Greek yogurt

2 tablespoons coconut milk

1 teaspoon salt

¼ cup panko breadcrumbs

¼ cup shredded coconut

Lime wedges for serving

DIRECTIONS

1 Spray air fryer rack or basket with cooking spray. Arrange fish in fryer.

2 In a small bowl, combine yogurt, coconut milk, and salt. In a separate bowl, combine breadcrumbs and shredded coconut. Generously brush fish with yogurt mixture. Divide crumb mixture among fillets, patting down to ensure it sticks.

3 Cook at 400°F for 10 to 12 minutes or until breading is golden brown and fish is cooked through.

4 Serve with lime wedges.

DILL PICKLE POTATO CHIP COD

SERVES 2

INGREDIENTS

- 2 tablespoons mayonnaise
- 2 teaspoons Dijon mustard
- Pepper
- 2 (6-ounce) cod fillets
- ½ cup crushed dill pickle potato chips
- Cooking spray

DIRECTIONS

1 Stir together the mayonnaise and mustard in a small bowl.Season cod fillets with pepper to taste, then spread mayonnaise mixture over the top of each cod fillet.

2 Divide crushed potato chips between fillets, pressing lightly into the mayonnaise mixture.

3 Preheat air fryer at 400°F for 2 minutes. Spray air fryer rack or basket with cooking spray. Carefully place fish in fryer. Cook at for 8 to 10 minutes or until fish flakes easily when tested with a fork.

ERIC SAYS: You can use any flavor chip or crispy snack for a different flavor profile. Nacho cheese chips and a side of salsa and crema will make this a Baja-style cod.

KETO BATTERED FISH & "CHIPS"

SERVES 4

INGREDIENTS

Cooking spray

½ cup unflavored protein powder

1 teaspoon salt

1½ teaspoons garlic powder

1 cup almond flour

4 teaspoons baking powder

2 large eggs

⅓ to ½ cup sparkling water, chilled

1 large eggplant, cut into 1×4-inch wedges

1½ pounds whitefish (cod or haddock), cut into 3×5-inch pieces

Lemon wedges, malt vinegar, and condiments for serving

DIRECTIONS

1 Spray air fryer racks or basket with cooking spray. In a medium bowl, combine protein powder, salt, garlic powder, almond flour, and baking powder.

2 In a separate large bowl, beat eggs. Gently pour in ⅓ cup sparkling water. Slowly fold in dry-ingredient mixture until all ingredients are combined, adding more sparkling water if necessary to achieve a medium-thick batter consistency.

3 Carefully dip eggplant wedges in the batter mixture. Place on fryer rack or in basket. (Be sure to not overcrowd.) Cook at 375°F for 12 to 15 minutes, or until golden brown. Repeat cooking process with any remaining wedges.

4 While eggplant fries are cooking, dip the fish in the batter mixture. Set aside until all eggplant wedges have been cooked.

5 Re-spray fryer rack or basket with cooking spray and place battered fish in fryer. Cook at 375°F for 10 to 15 minutes, flipping halfway through cooking time.

6 Serve fish and chips with lemon wedges, malt vinegar, and desired condiments for dipping.

SPICY SHRIMP FAJITA RICE BOWLS

SERVES 4

INGREDIENTS

- ½ cup olive oil
- ½ cup chopped fresh cilantro, divided
- ½ cup fresh lime juice, divided
- 1 tablespoon hot sauce
- ½ teaspoon cayenne (optional)
- 1 teaspoon ground cumin
- 3 cloves, minced
- 1 pound shrimp, fresh or frozen, thawed, peeled and deveined, tails removed
- 3 cups or red and/or green sliced sweet peppers
- 1 cup thinly sliced red onion
- 2 cups water
- 1 cup long-grain white rice
- 2 cups canned black beans, drained and rinsed
- 2 cups corn kernels
- 1 avocado, pitted and sliced
- Sour cream, sliced scallions, and lime wedges for garnish

DIRECTIONS

1 In a large sealable freezer bag, combine oil, ¼ cup cilantro, ¼ cup lime juice, hot sauce, cayenne, if using, cumin, and garlic. Add shrimp, peppers, and onions to the marinade. Seal and marinate in the refrigerator for 1 hour.

2 Meanwhile, bring water, remaining lime juice, and rice to a boil in a medium saucepan. Reduce heat to low. Cover and cook for 14 to 15 minutes or until rice is cooked through and liquid has evaporated. Fluff with a fork, stir in remaining cilantro, and keep warm until serving time.

3 Drain shrimp mixture thoroughly and arrange on air fryer rack or in basket. Cook at 375° F for 6 to 8 minutes, stirring or shaking the basket halfway through the cooking time, until peppers and onions are lightly browned and shrimp are pink.

4 To assemble, divide rice among four bowls. Top one half of rice with shrimp mixture. Top other half with beans in one quarter and corn in remaining quarter.

5 Fan avocado slices on top. Garnish with dollop of sour cream and a sprinkle of scallions. Serve with lime wedges.

> **ERIC SAYS:** If you want to save some time, you can get precooked heat-and-eat rice. Heat according to directions, then add lime juice and cilantro to taste.

HOW SWEET IS THIS?
DESSERTS

S'MORES IN A CAKE CONE

SERVES 6

INGREDIENTS

½ cup milk chocolate chips
cones

1 cup mini marshmallows

½ cup graham cracker
crumbs

6 cake-style ice cream
cones

6 maraschino cherries

Optional Toppings:

¼ cup chopped dried fruit

¼ cup chopped peanuts

Fudge sauce, for
drizzling

DIRECTIONS

1 Divide the chocolate chips, marshmallows, and graham cracker crumbs into thirds. Layer them in a total of nine layers in the cones following order: chocolate chips, graham cracker crumbs, and marshmallows, piling the final layer of marshmallows on top as high as you can.

2 Place the cones standing upright on the air fryer rack. (For added stability, place each cone in a coffee cup or espresso cup.) Cook at 375°F for 4 to 6 minutes, or until the marshmallows are nicely browned. Let cool.

3 When cooled enough to handle, top with cherries and add optional toppings, if desired.

BAKLAVA BITES

MAKES 20

INGREDIENTS

- 1 egg
- 2 tablespoons light corn syrup
- 2 tablespoons honey
- 2 tablespoons brown sugar
- 1 tablespoon all-purpose flour
- ½ teaspoon cinnamon
- ½ teaspoon vanilla extract
- ⅓ cup finely chopped walnuts, pecans, or pistachios
- 20 mini phyllo pastry shells

DIRECTIONS

1 In a bowl, whisk together the egg, corn syrup, honey, brown sugar, flour, cinnamon, and vanilla. Stir in the nuts. Divide filling among pastry shells.

2 Preheat air fryer at 375°F for 2 minutes. Carefully place the filled pastry shells in air fryer. Cook at 375°F for 6 minutes.

3 Using tongs, remove bites from fryer and let cool.

ERIC SAYS: I love to "a la mode" these crispy bites and serve with French vanilla ice cream and a drizzle of more honey on top. A good strong espresso will complete the treat.

INDIVIDUAL KEY LIME PIES WITH COCONUT STREUSEL

MAKES 6

INGREDIENTS

2 egg yolks

¾ cup sweetened condensed milk

¼ cup lime juice

2 teaspoons lime zest

6 mini graham cracker pie crusts

3 tablespoons sweetened flaked coconut

2 tablespoons sugar

2 tablespoons all-purpose flour

2 teaspoons melted butter

Whipped cream for garnish (optional)

DIRECTIONS

1 In a small bowl, whisk together the egg yolks, sweetened condensed milk, lime juice, and lime zest. Divide the filling among pie crusts. In a separate bowl, combine the coconut, sugar, flour, and butter. Mix until crumbly. Top each pie with the coconut mixture.

2 If using an oven-style fryer, place 3 pies on each rack. If using a basket-style fryer, cook 3 pies at a time. Cook pies at 320°F for 10 minutes, rotating racks after 5 minutes. Remove pies and let cool.

3 Serve with whipped cream, if desired.

ERIC SAYS: Don't be afraid to make seasonal changes to this recipe. I've used clementines, tangerines, and even ruby red grapefruit.

FLOURLESS CHOCOLATE CAKE WITH RASPBERRY GANACHE

SERVES 8 TO 10

INGREDIENTS

FOR THE CAKE

Cooking spray or softened butter for greasing pan

½ cup butter, cut into chunks

6 ounces semi-sweet chocolate, broken into pieces

⅔ cup sugar

4 eggs

1½ teaspoons vanilla extract

⅓ cup cocoa powder

½ teaspoon baking powder

Pinch of salt

FOR THE GANACHE

3 ounces semi-sweet chocolate, broken in pieces

3 tablespoons heavy cream

3 tablespoons seedless raspberry jam

1 tablespoon butter

DIRECTIONS

1 For the cake: Grease an 8-inch round cake pan with cooking spray or butter. Line the greased pan with parchment paper, then grease the parchment paper. Set aside.

2 In a medium-size microwave safe bowl, melt chocolate and butter in 20 second increments, stirring after each increment until completely melted and smooth. Whisk in the sugar, eggs, and vanilla extract. Whisk in the cocoa powder, baking powder, and salt, blending well.

3 Preheat air fryer at 350°F for 2 minutes. Using an oven mitt, place cake in fryer and cook 350°F for 30 minutes. Allow cake to rest in the air fryer for 15 minutes.

4 Meanwhile, make the ganache: In a microwave-safe bowl, combine chocolate, heavy cream, jam, and butter. Melt in 20 second increments, stirring after each increment until completely melted and smooth.

5 Using an oven mitt, remove the cake from the air fryer and let cool 20 minutes on a wire rack. When cool enough to handle, run a knife around the edge of the cake. Invert cake onto a serving plate and refrigerate for 1 hour.

6 Spread ganache over the top of the refrigerated cake and place back into the refrigerator for another 1 to 2 hours before serving.

> **ERIC SAYS:** I prefer a Kentucky Coffee with this cake. Hot coffee, sugar, and bourbon topped with a little whipped cream......yum!!!

OREO® MARSHMALLOW PIE

SERVES 6 TO 8

INGREDIENTS

- 8 ounces milk chocolate morsels
- 6 ounces semi-sweet chocolate morsels
- ¾ cup heavy whipping cream
- 1 prepared Oreo® pie crust
- ¼ cup graham cracker crumbs
- ¼ cup chopped peanuts
- 12 jumbo marshmallows, cut in half

DIRECTIONS

1 Combine milk chocolate and semi-sweet morsels in a medium bowl. In a small pan, bring the cream to a boil, then turn off the heat. Pour hot cream over the chips. Stir until smooth.

2 Pour chocolate-cream mixture into the crust, then sprinkle graham cracker crumbs and peanuts evenly over the top. Cover with foil or plastic wrap and place in the refrigerator for at least 4 hours.

3 When chocolate has set up and is firm, arrange marshmallows in concentric circles on top of the pie, covering as much of the filling as possible. Don't be afraid to crowd them. Cook at 400°F for 1 to 2 minutes or until marshmallows are golden brown. (Set the timer for 1-minute increments so you don't burn the marshmallows!)

4 Cool pie until filling is not runny, about 5 minutes, before serving.

ERIC SAYS: As if this wasn't decadent enough, hot chocolate spiked with coffee liqueur will take it over the top!

CHERRY-ALMOND CLAFOUTIS

SERVES 6 TO 8

INGREDIENTS

- ⅓ cup sliced almonds
- 2 cups frozen pitted sweet cherries, thawed
- 2 teaspoons butter, room temperature, plus 1 tablespoon butter, melted
- 1 cup milk
- ⅔ cup all-purpose flour
- ¼ cup sugar
- ¼ cup heavy cream
- 3 eggs
- ¼ teaspoon almond extract
- Powdered sugar for dusting

DIRECTIONS

1 Line an air fryer rack or basket with foil. Spread the almonds over foil and toast at 350°F for 4 to 6 minutes, stirring or tossing periodically. Remove almonds from air fryer and set aside to cool.

2 Grease the bottom of an 8-inch nonstick cake pan with 2 teaspoons butter. Place cherries in the greased pan.

3 In a bowl, whisk together the milk, flour, sugar, heavy cream, eggs, 1 tablespoon melted butter, and almond extract. Pour mixture over cherries.

4 Cook at 350°F for 20 to 25 minutes. To ensure that the cake is fully cooked, insert a toothpick into the center and if it comes out clean, its cooked. When finished, the cake should be puffy and golden brown.

5 Using an oven mitt, remove pan and let cool to room temperature. Garnish top of cake with toasted almonds and a dusting of powdered sugar.

> **ERIC SAYS:** This recipe was created to feature stone fruit. Fresh and seasonal peaches, plums, or apricots are amazing substitutes for the cherries. I also like to serve with a side of vanilla cream sauce.

CHOCOLATE-CHERRY BOMBS

MAKES 10

INGREDIENTS

1 (7.5-ounce) tube refrigerated biscuits

10 mini cream-fillled chocolate cookies

10 small squares milk chocolate bar

10 maraschino cherries, drained and patted dry

Cooking spray

3 tablespoons sugar

½ teaspoon cinnamon

3 tablespoons butter

DIRECTIONS

1 Remove biscuits from tube and press into flat discs. Layer 1 mini chocolate cookie, 1 chocolate square, and 1 maraschino cherry in the center of each biscuit. Fold and pinch the edges of the biscuits around all of the ingredients, making sure there are no holes.

2 Spray air fryer racks or basket with cooking spray. Cook biscuits at 395ºF for 8 to 10 minutes, or until golden brown. Let cool until cool enough to handle.

3 In a small bowl, mix together sugar and cinnamon. Melt butter in a microwave-safe bowl in the microwave. Brush biscuits with butter, then roll in cinnamon-sugar mixture. Serve warm.

ERIC SAYS: Don't be afraid to switch the biscuits for croissant or phyllo dough. It doesn't hurt to serve with extra chocolate sauce on the side for dipping!

ERIC SAYS: Don't be afraid to switch the biscuits for croissant or phyllo dough. It doesn't hurt to serve with extra chocolate sauce on the side for dipping!

ROASTED STRAWBERRY-CHOCOLATE CHIP SHORTCAKE

SERVES 4

INGREDIENTS

Parchment paper

1¾ cup all-purpose baking mix

⅓ cup + 3 tablespoons milk

½ cup mini chocolate chips

2 pounds strawberries, stemmed and halved

2 tablespoons sugar

1 teaspoon vanilla extract

1 teaspoon lemon juice

⅛ teaspoon salt

Whipped cream for serving

DIRECTIONS

1 Line air fryer rack or basket with parchment paper.

2 In a medium bowl, combine baking mix, milk, and chocolate chips. Gently mix until ingredients are blended. Shape into four shortcakes.

3 Preheat air fryer to 375°F for 2 minutes. Place shortcakes in fryer and cook for 10 to 12 minutes or until golden brown. Remove from fryer and cool on a wire rack.

4 Combine strawberries, sugar, vanilla, lemon juice, and salt in a heat-proof dish that fits in the air fryer. Allow to stand for 10 minutes.

5 Cook strawberries for 8 minutes at 400°F, stirring halfway through the cooking time. Using an oven mitt, carefully remove from air fryer.

6 Slice shortcakes in half horizontally. Spoon warm strawberries over each shortcake bottom and place shortcake on top.

7 Serve with whipped cream.

> **ERIC SAYS:** When I think about strawberries and chocolate, I think about a champagne cocktail with orange liqueur. Definitely a romantic pairing!

BANANA-CHOCOLATE CHIP COFFEE CAKE

SERVES 6 TO 8

INGREDIENTS

FOR THE TOPPING

½ cup all-purpose flour

¼ cup packed brown sugar

½ teaspoon cinnamon

3 tablespoon cold butter, cut into cubes

FOR THE COFFEE CAKE

2 very ripe bananas, about ¾ cup mashed

1 tablespoon butter, melted

2 tablespoon plain yogurt

¼ cup sugar

1 egg

½ teaspoon vanilla

½ cup all-purpose flour

¼ cup whole wheat flour

½ teaspoon baking soda

½ teaspoon cinnamon

Pinch of salt

⅓ cup mini chocolate chips

Cooking spray

DIRECTIONS

1 For the topping: In a small bowl combine the flour, brown sugar, and cinnamon. Cut in the butter with a pastry blender or two butter knives until crumbly. Set aside.

2 For the coffee cake: In a large bowl, combine the mashed bananas, butter, yogurt, sugar, egg, and vanilla.

3 In a medium bowl, combine both flours, baking soda, cinnamon, and salt. Add dry ingredients to wet ingredients, gently folding together until combined. Fold in chocolate chips.

4 Spray a 7-inch nonstick round cake pan with cooking spray. Pour batter into the pan. Spread topping over the surface of the cake.

5 Preheat air fryer at 350°F for 2 minutes. Place cake in fryer and cook for 25 to 30 minutes, or until a toothpick inserted in the center of the cake comes out clean.

ERIC SAYS: If you like extra topping, like me—and if you like coconut— add a ½ cup shredded coconut to the topping mixture!

PIÑA COLADA UPSIDE-DOWN CAKES

MAKES 2

INGREDIENTS

Cooking spray

¼ cup cream of coconut, divided

2 pineapple rings, fresh or canned

2 stemless maraschino cherries

1 egg

2 tablespoons butter, melted

½ teaspoon vanilla extract

1½ tablespoons milk

¼ cup all-purpose flour

¼ teaspoon baking powder

⅓ cup sweetened coconut flakes

Pinch of salt

DIRECTIONS

1 Spray two 12-ounce ramekins with cooking spray.

2 Place 1 tablespoon cream of coconut in each ramekin. Place 1 pineapple ring on top of the cream and 1 maraschino cherry in the center of each ring.

3 In a bowl, combine whisk together the egg, remaining 2 tablespoons cream of coconut, butter, vanilla extract, and milk. Stir in the flour, baking powder, coconut flakes, and salt. Divide batter equally between the ramekins.

4 Preheat air fryer for 2 minutes at 350°F. Place ramekins in fryer. Cook for 15 minutes.

5 Using an oven mitt, remove the cakes from fryer and let cool for 10 to 15 minutes.

6 When cool enough to hold, invert the cakes onto plates and serve.

> **ERIC SAYS:** Change it up a little and throw in a few fresh blueberries instead of the cherry if they are in season. Don't forget the spiced rum whipped cream!

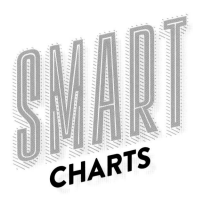

CHARTS

Dry (Weight) Measurements

MISC.*	TEASPOONS	TABLESPOONS	OUNCES	CUPS	GRAMS	POUNDS
1 dash	¹⁄₁₆ tsp.	-	-	-	-	-
1 pinch / 6 drops	⅛ tsp.	-	-	-	-	-
15 drops	¼ tsp.	-	-	-	-	-
1 splash	½ tsp.	-	-	-	-	-
-	1 tsp.	⅓ tbsp.	⅙ oz	-	-	-
-	3 tsp.	1 tbsp.	½ oz	-	14.3 g	-
-	-	2 tbsp.	1 oz	⅛ cup	28.3 g	-
-	-	4 tbsp.	2 oz	¼ cup	56.7 g	-
-	-	5 ⅓ tbsp.	2.6 oz	⅓ cup	75.6 g	-
-	-	8 tbsp.	4 oz	½ cup	113.4 g	-
-	-	12 tbsp.	6 oz	¾ cup	170.1 g	-
-	-	16 tbsp.	8 oz	1 cup	226.8 g	½ lb
-	-	32 tbsp.	16 oz	2 cups	453.6 g	1 lb
-	-	64 tbsp.	32 oz	4 cups / 1 qt.	907.2 g	2 lb

Abbreviations

TERM	DRY & LIQUID	ABBREVIATION
cup	usually liquid	-
fluid ounce	only liquid	fl oz.
gallon	dry or liquid	-
inch	-	in.
ounce	dry	oz.
pint	dry or liquid	-
pound	dry	lb
quart	dry or liquid	qt./qts.
teaspoon	dry or liquid	tsp.
tablespoon	dry or liquid	tbsp.

Liquid (Volume) Measurements

FLUID OUNCES	TABLESPOONS	CUPS	MILLILITER/ LITERS	PINTS	QUARTS	GALLONS
1 fl oz	2 tbsp.	⅛ cup	30 ml	-	-	-
2 fl oz	4 tbsp.	¼ cup	60 ml	-	-	-
4 fl oz	8 tbsp.	½ cup	125 ml	-	-	
8 fl oz	16 tbsp.	1 cup	250 ml	-	-	-
12 fl oz	-	1½ cups	375 ml	-	-	-
16 fl oz	-	2 cups	500 ml	1 pint	-	-
32 fl oz	-	4 cups	1 L	2 pints	1 qt.	-
128 fl oz	-	16 cups	4 L	8 pints	4 qts.	1 gallon

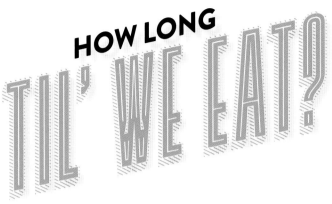

HOW LONG TIL' WE EAT?

Safe steps in food handling, cooking, and storage are essential for preventing foodborne illness. You can't see, smell, or taste harmful bacteria that may cause illness.

Cook all food to these minimum internal temperatures as measured with a food thermometer before removing food from the heat source. Let rest for a minimum of 10 mins. before serving unless indicated otherwise.

In every step of food preparation, follow the four guidelines to help keep food safe:
Clean—Wash hands and surfaces often.
Separate—Separate raw meat from other foods.
Cook—Cook to the right temperature.
Chill—Refrigerate food promptly.

Cooking Temperature Charts

DONENESS	SERVING TEMPERATURE ERIC'S RECOMMENDATION	SERVING TEMPERATURE USDA'S RECOMMENDATION
Beef, Lamb, Pork, Veal Steaks, Chops & Roasts		
Rare	125°F (52°C)	*
Medium Rare	130°F (54°C)	*
Medium	135°F (57°C)	Minimum Internal Temperature & Rest Time: 145°F (63°C) and allow to rest for at least 3 mins.
Medium Well	150° F (65°C)	
Well Done	150°F (over 65°C)	

* Consuming raw or undercooked meats, poultry, seafood, shellfish, or eggs may increase your risk of foodborne illness. http://fsis.usda.gov/

DONENESS	SERVING TEMPERATURE ERIC'S RECOMMENDATION	SERVING TEMPERATURE USDA'S RECOMMENDATION
Ground Meats, Burgers, Meatloaf & Sausages Except Poultry		
Recommended	160°F (71°C)	Minimum Internal Temperature: 160°F (71°C)*
Burgers (Beef)		
Recommended	140°F (60°C)	160°F (71°C)
Pork Ribs, Pork Shoulders		
Tender and Juicy	180-190°F (82-88°C)	*
Precooked Ham		
Recommended	140°F (60°C)	Reheat cooked hams packaged in USDA-inspected plants to 140°F (60°C); all others to 165° F (74°C)*
Turkey & Chicken, Whole or Ground		
Recommended	165°F (74°C)	Minimum Internal Temperature: 165°F (74°C)*
Fish		
Rare	125°F (52°C)	*
Medium	135°F (57°C)	*
Well Done	145°F (63°C)	Minimum Internal Temperature: 145°F (63°C)*
Unpasteurized Eggs		
Recommended	160°F (71°C)	Minimum Internal Temperature: 160°F (71°C)*

* Consuming raw or undercooked meats, poultry, seafood, shellfish, or eggs may increase your risk of foodborne illness. http://fsis.usda.gov/

ERIC'S FAVORITE RUBS

POUNDIN' THE FOOD WITH FLAVOR

These are my go-to rubs that add an extra punch of "wow" to anything that you're preparing. Each recipe yields about ½ cup and should be stored in small air-tight containers. Making extra rubs saves time and money, and you will enjoy having some versatile flavors ready to use in your cooking arsenal.

Rubs are great for meat, fish, and poultry—you can even season a salad with the Everyday Rub. Try the Poultry Rub on grilled veggies. The Red Meat Rub is great for flavoring your meatloaf or adding to a pot of chili. And for savory fries or popcorn, try the Seasoned Salt mix.

DIRECTIONS: Mix all the ingredients together until well incorporated. You can make into a fine powder by placing into a blender or spice grinder.

POULTRY

- 2 tablespoons crushed sea salt
- 2 tablespoons paprika
- 1 teaspoon sugar
- 1 tablespoon turmeric
- 2 teaspoons garlic powder
- 2 teaspoons granulated dried onion
- 1 tablespoon ground thyme
- 1 teaspoon mustard powder
- ½ teaspoon cayenne
- 2 teaspoons dried lemon peel
- 1 tablespoon black ground pepper

EVERYDAY

- 2 tablespoons crushed sea salt
- 2 tablespoons crushed black pepper
- 2 tablespoons granulated garlic
- 2 tablespoons granulated onion
- 1 tablespoon dried basil
- ½ teaspoon red pepper flakes
- 1 tablespoon coriander
- 1 teaspoon dry mustard
- 1 teaspoon brown sugar

FISH

- 1 tablespoon crushed sea salt
- 1 tablespoon onion powder
- 1 teaspoon thyme
- 2 teaspoons tarragon
- 1 tablespoon dried parsley
- 1 tablespoon dried chives
- 1 tablespoon ground white pepper
- 1 tablespoon dried lemon peel
- 1 teaspoon celery seed

RED MEAT

- 2 tablespoons crushed sea salt
- 2 tablespoons brown sugar
- 2 tablespoons ground black coffee
- 1 tablespoon granulated garlic
- 1 tablespoon granulated onion
- 1 tablespoon cumin
- 1 tablespoon coriander
- 1 tablespoon freshly ground black pepper

SEASONED SALT

- 1 cup coarse ground sea salt
- ¼ cup black peppercorns
- 3 sprigs rosemary
- 4 sprigs thyme
- 2 sprigs sage
- 3 sprigs tarragon
- 1 clove garlic, peeled

INDEX

Also available from Eric Theiss

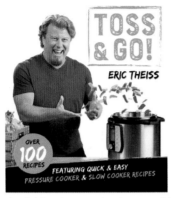

Available wherever books are sold.

A POST HILL PRESS BOOK
ISBN: 978-1-63758-328-9
ISBN (eBook): 978-1-63758-329-6

Lovin' Your Air Fryer:
110 Fast & Easy Recipes for Mornin' to Late-Night Munchin'
© 2022 by Eric Theiss
All Rights Reserved

Cover and interior photography, by Ken Carlson

Post Hill
PRESS

Post Hill Press
New York • Nashville
posthillpress.com

Published in the United States of America

1 2 3 4 5 6 7 8 9 10